T0303362

THE *(Inter)* NATIONAL
BASKETBALL
ASSOCIATION

THE *(Inter)* NATIONAL BASKETBALL ASSOCIATION

How the NBA Ushered in a New Era of Basketball and Went Global

JOEL GUNDERSON

Afterword by **TYLER SMITH**

Sports Publishing books may be purchased in bulk at special discounts for sales promotion, corporate gifts, fund-raising, or educational purposes. Special editions can also be created to specifications. For details, contact the Special Sales Department, Sports Publishing, 307 West 36th Street, 11th Floor, New York, NY 10018 or sportspubbooks@skyhorsepublishing.com.

Sports Publishing® is a registered trademark of Skyhorse Publishing, Inc.®, a Delaware corporation.

Visit our website at www.sportspubbooks.com.

10 9 8 7 6 5 4 3 2 1

Library of Congress Cataloging-in-Publication Data is available on file.

Cover design by Brian Peterson
Cover photo credits: Getty Images

Print ISBN: 978-1-68358-348-6
Ebook ISBN: 978-1-68358-349-3

Printed in the United States of America

Dedicated to my Grandma Schurr, who sat through hours of my retellings of Blazers games gone by.

I'm sending a copy up to you in spirit.

CONTENTS

CONTENTS

Preface

On the morning of January 26, 2020, I was sitting in our newly designed reading nook near the back of our house. My wife and I had recently converted it from our kids' old playroom, which is a nice way of saying we converted it from an area most reminiscent to "The Island of Misfit Toys."

After feeding the kids their breakfast and then cleaning up their peanut butter and jelly faces, I had settled into the chair nestled near the back window of the house, which overlooked our backyard, which itself bled into the neighborhood park. My wife was out with our oldest daughter, enjoying some mother-daughter time. And shopping, of course.

It was a rare sunny January day in Oregon; the unrelenting rain had slipped away, leaving behind flocks of chirping birds. The sounds of kids sprung free from the shackles of winter reverberated from the park. The shadows of the trees danced all around me, making the words on the pages of my book almost impossible to absorb, but entrancing all the same.

It was one of those perfect, tranquil days when you wonder why you ever let emotions get the best of you.

Between sips of coffee and unmet requests to my kids to keep their volume down, I was finding myself gazing outside more than normal. Perhaps it was the sun. Perhaps it was the post-run high that lingered; I was in that blissful moment in time before my dopamine levels settled back to reality. But for some reason, the moments were slowing more than usual, and I felt as if I was slowing down with it, absorbing the scene around more than I normally had.

The time was 1:07 p.m. PST.

When I flipped over my phone and pressed the home button, I instinctively pulled up Twitter. From there, my reactions came in waves, just like every other person around the globe, who was seeing the news as well.

Kobe Bryant was dead.

Over the course of the next hour or two, then three and four, as the news was absorbed, then disbelieved, then confirmed, I dove headfirst into the world's reactions. What was striking me—someone who had never met Kobe, not even in my time covering the NBA as a freelance reporter—wasn't so much the outpouring from former teammates and rivals alike, but from people long removed from Kobe himself. Childhood schoolmates. Teammates from third grade. Teachers who recalled the small child with the big smile and even bigger bubble of confidence. Neighbors from the countries and cities Kobe had called home during his life: Italy, Philadelphia, and Los Angeles.

"Kobe was very serious and very professional. Even when he was ten or eleven years old, he had the 'Mamba mentality,'" said childhood friend and former teammate Davide Giudici, referring to the phrase Bryant coined to describe his winning attitude. "I was shocked, totally shocked. My first thought is about his family, his wife, sisters, his daughters. I was very sad thinking about Kobe at that moment."

Kobe's global presence had been felt since his star took off in the mid-1990s, but his upbringing in Italy—he moved to Rieti in 1984 when his father, Joe "Jellybean" Bryant, signed with the AMG Sebastiani Rieti—was always at the root of who he was as a person. His on-court presence was "Black Mamba," a man driven to rip your soul out in the most painful manner. His off-court demeanor, however, was all Italy.

Family. Giving. Gregarious. Loud.

Italy.

* * *

I grew up a stone's throw from Portland, Oregon, now the lone professional basketball franchise in the Pacific Northwest. From the first breaths my body drew in this world, I was enamored with the Portland Trail Blazers. They absorbed me; to this day, its clutches have never fully let go. As life moves onward, I've grown up (as people do). I've gotten married, had three kids, and accumulated hobbies and responsibilities (as people also do). But the passion for my first love never left. When the Blazers are playing, and I can steal a moment or two, I'm watching. When I have a break at work, I'm scouring the Internet for any news—good or bad—that pertains to them.

When you're young and impressionable—and, perhaps most, emotional—it's easy to take things personal that have no business of being that way.

When it came to my childhood Blazers fandom, I, of course, worshipped the players who donned our uniforms. Clyde Drexler. Terry Porter. Jerome Kersey. Perhaps most of all, because of the headband (back when it was still unusual), Cliff "Uncle Cliffy"

Robinson. These men towered over me both in height and stature. But outside of Portland, those who wore jerseys that I disagreed with became my enemies; men sent to destroy my team's destiny. Two men stuck out most. The first was the immortalized-but-hated-in-my-house Michael Jordan. The 1992 NBA Finals cemented that.

But the second? That was Kobe Bryant.

As my early years came and went, I often felt like the only kid my age who looked at Michael Jordan, the living embodiment of perfection and worship to most, and *despised* him. I despised him for everything he did to *my* team; for everything he did to your team, too, but I didn't mind that as much. But too often he crushed the spirit of *my* team.

I cried crocodile tears when he shrugged after hitting yet another three-pointer in the 1992 NBA Finals. Then, I cried tears of joy when he retired a year later. I was elated then, five years after that, when he hung them up for the second time. By the time he returned in the blue and white of the Washington Wizards, still dangerous but hardly the liquidator he had been years prior, a new enemy had arrived.

Jordan was irrelevant by then, an old man in an ambiguous franchise, far removed from my concerns.

The new enemy, though?

He was new. He was fresh. He was just as confident as Jordan had been in his prime. He was just as strong-willed in his desire to be the best as Jordan had been.

And, much like Jordan had all those years prior, he seemed to take great pleasure in puncturing our sails.

The position of Blazers-killer had been filled by Kobe Bryant.

From the moment he donned the purple and gold in the summer of 1996, his fate with me was sealed. Because if Jordan was the heel in my body, the Los Angeles Lakers were that in my soul. Partly due to proximity, partly due to the vengeful battles waged, the Lakers were the antithesis of everything I adored about those Blazers squads of my youth. The Lakers were swag, sex, money, and titles. Those Blazers were subtlety, suburban marriage, and the ever-so-closeness of second place.

The Lakers were flash and popularity. The Blazers were substance and uncool.

And Kobe, crooked smile and smirk, was the *perfect* Laker.

* * *

The year 2000 was set up perfectly for my beloved Trail Blazers. The franchise had made all of the right moves the previous couple of offseason, expanding the fever of the fan base. The roster was overflowing with talent and experience. Scottie Pippen, Jordan's long-time running mate who had played no small part in our previous failures, had signed on as (hopefully) the final piece to the puzzle. It had been eight seasons since Portland had made the NBA Finals; twenty-three years since their lone championship in the summer of 1977.

And as it was meant to be, as Portland made it to the Western Conference finals, where they would face a Lakers squad featuring Shaquille O'Neal, Kobe, and Phil Jackson, the sports world ground to a halt to zero in on the rebirthed rivalry. The two teams would, in fact, engage in arguably the most entertaining, hard-fought, emotional, draining series the sport had seen in decades. Every game was played with the fervor ratcheted up to unsustainable levels.

The city of Portland was never more passionate. Even Los Angeles, a town often bereft of zealousness, was fully invested. The NBA would fulcrum on the series living up to the seasons-long prediction and hype, and it delivered.

I was inside the Rose Garden for Game Six, when the Blazers pulled away late, forcing a seventh game in Los Angeles that coming Sunday. I sang as loud as anyone when, late in the fourth quarter and the victory all but secured, Jack Nicholson—the longest-tenured and most visible Lakers celebrity endorser—stood up and made his exit from the arena, 20,000 people serenading him with the song "Hit the Road Jack."

I still get goosebumps recalling the scene as fans chanted in the corridor after the game, in unison, alongside high-fives and hugs among strangers, "Beat LA! Beat LA!"

I remember the things I said both in my head and out loud that coming Sunday afternoon when Kobe lobbed the ball to Shaq for the dunk that ended my innocence, ushering in pain and misery that I had yet to experience. I said unforgivable things about a man I had never met, who was not much older than myself, but lived in a world I could not fathom.

I hated him. I hated Kobe Bryant.

I wanted to never see him again. I loathed the smile and the way he wore his hair. I hated the jersey he wore, and what he did to me and my team.

I carried that torch for the next sixteen years, but it would slowly dampen over time. Both Kobe and I made mistakes in our lives; we put ourselves in compromising positions that were hard to traverse. We both got married and had baby girls. He didn't get to experience the connection of a baby boy like I did, so that was one thing I had over him.

By the time he had retired in 2016, my unfiltered hatred had morphed into a feeling of *meh*. As I hit my thirties, I didn't have the energy to carry those negative torches in my life. By that point, Kobe had gone from the man I most opposed, to a man I simply watched.

* * *

"He was my idol. Not just my idol, but also to a generation of people my age," Giannis Antetokounmpo, arguably the NBA's biggest star, said before the 2020 NBA All-Star Game in Chicago, less than one month after Bryant's death. "He was one of those guys who gave back to the game so much, gave back to the players so much. A lot of times the great ones don't do that. It was important to him. He said that talent was worthless if you're not willing to share it, and he was one of those guys who would share it with us. He's going to be missed."

Giannis was in Athens, Greece, almost 7,000 miles away from the epicenter, when Kobe lobbed the ball to Shaq in the summer of 2000. He was just five years old, with no true connection to the NBA. This was long before anyone could hop on YouTube and watch highlights of their favorite player; before he could scroll through his phone to see stats or highlights. In an interview with the *Greek Reporter* after Bryant's death, Giannis discusses the effect that Bryant had on his approach:

> How did Kobe inspire me? Just work hard, be fearless, don't really care about what people have to say about you, just go out there and do your job, have a smile on your face. You're going to have to sacrifice a lot, a lot of family time, obviously, to play this game, but your family knows why you were put on this Earth, why you play this game, which is to provide for them because that's what you're born to do. Kobe means greatness. . . . He always had that smile, he always had that charisma that he carried with him. I think it touched a lot of people in the world. It's going to be hard for another basketball player to view me as I view Kobe. [He] was one of the best basketball players to play the game. He was put on this Earth to be one of

the best. When I'm gone, if I can impact people's lives the way Kobe impacted mine and people's lives around the world, that would be a blessing.

Word of what Kobe, or Ken Griffey Jr., or Peyton Manning, or any other sports star were accomplishing had long ways to travel. Perhaps, because of that, the impact of what those stars were able to accomplish hit harder to a younger generation. With the lack of access, players like Kobe were larger than life, more so than players today could ever be.

"[That day] was a horrible day for basketball, for everybody. A lot of people were really affected by it. I send my deepest condolences to their family, Vanessa and the kids that they leave behind," Antetokounmpo said. "All I can do is pray for them."

* * *

For the local folks back in Italy, where Kobe's name still rang in the halls like a long-ago son not yet returned, the news of his death on January 26, 2020, tore through a bit harder. When Kobe, his daughter Gianna, and seven other people fell from the sky that morning, the country had lost one of their own, if by osmosis only.

"All of the NBA players are important, because they're legends, but he's particularly important to us because he knew Italy so well, having lived in several cities here," Italian Basketball Federation president Giovanni Petrucci told the Associated Press after Bryant's death. "He had a lot of Italian qualities. He spoke Italian very well. He even knew the local slang."

"He was a supernatural," Italian coach Ettore Messina, who worked with Bryant as an assistant for the Lakers, told the AP. "To hear him speak and joke in our language and to remember when his father played here, and he was a kid drew a lot of people to the NBA. He was also always very attentive to help Italian kids arriving in the NBA and to help them enter such a tough and competitive world. He also did that with me when I arrived at the Lakers and I'm still very grateful to him for that. It's very sad that his family has been devastated like this."

Although the majority of his basketball career took place in the United States, Kobe's love of the game, and his drive for perfection, were birthed in Italy. It's where his formative years, when the brain is its most absorbent and your surroundings seep into your subconscious, driving him to be who he would later become.

"Italy is my home. It's where my dream of playing in the NBA started. This is where I learned the fundamentals, learned to shoot, to pass and to [move] without the ball," Bryant once the *Gazzetta dello Sport*, Italy's top sports newspaper, "All things that when I came back to America the players my age didn't know how to do because they were only thinking about jumping and dunking."

Tragic news enters your mind in obscure ways. No one quite knows how they'll handle it, since it's not something you can prepare for. It's a visceral feeling, organic to each individual scenario. When *TMZ* first reported that Kobe had passed, a world waited for finality.

Was it true?

It can't be true.

It must be true.

There's no way it's true.

Almost immediately after the first tweet went live that something tragic had happened, the hashtag #Eternal4a.m. also went viral, reflecting the time when news of the death became known in China. It was also symbolic for Bryant, who one time answered a reporter's question about the secret of his success: "Have you ever seen Los Angeles at 4 a.m.?"

"I've never seen Los Angeles at 4 a.m., but I heard the news of your death at 4 a.m.," thousands of fans posted.

Following his death, the Italian Basketball Federation declared the entire week be dedicated to their former son. Before every game that followed over the next seven days—regardless of what level the game was played at—one full minute of silence took place before the action in remembrance of Bryant, his daughter Gigi, and all of those aboard the helicopter.

"It's a small but heartfelt and deserved gesture to honor the life and memory of Kobe Bryant, an absolute champion who always had Italy in his heart," the federation said at the time. "Kobe was and will always be linked to our country."

In the spirit of the Italian manner, where friends are family, and family is something more than blood, the *Gazzetta dello Sport*, rounded up all of the emotions felt worldwide, from Los Angeles to New York, to London, Italy, and beyond, when their headline, following the news of Bryant's passing, came simple and poignant:

"We've Lost a Friend."

* * *

Back at my home, as it did at yours, the sun rose the next day, January 27. My children straggled out of bed. They brushed their teeth, slipped on their clothes, and went about their day, blissfully ignorant of the prior days' events. There's beauty in youth in moments of pain—their brains cannot yet compute the finality of death. To them, it's not a forever goodbye.

Because of that innocence, they don't understand the grip sports can carry on a person. They don't yet know what it's like to love or loathe someone based on the color of their jersey, the city they play in, or the way the sun beams off the top of their helmet as they burst through the tunnel. They have yet to feel the weightlessness of a walk-off win, or the empty feeling that rolls around the bottom of your stomach when it goes wrong.

I was sadder the morning after Kobe's death than I had been in some time. My joints felt burdened. I felt grief for Kobe and his family, like others, but I felt guilt, too. Guilt for carrying that hatred toward him for so long. Hatred that I harbored for ... what? An eighteen-year-old kid who just wanted to play basketball and was taken by a team I didn't like? That's why I hated him? He did nothing to me or my family. He was a young man living out his dream, outworking us all, to climb the mountain in his quest to become one of the greatest to ever do something he loved.

That morning I felt disappointment for not allowing myself to appreciate what was unfolding in front of me for all those years that followed: Kobe's greatness in motion, a greatness that's hard to replicate, and a uniqueness which we may not see for a long time. I felt disappointment for taking for granted a player that I undoubtedly would have worshipped had he been wearing our colors and not theirs.

The pain of those losses in the early 2000s was now more a bad memory than anything else. But what saddened me the most the day after his death, as countless tales of his gifts as a father began to overshadow his gifts as a basketball player, was that my blindness toward him had robbed me of valuable lessons he could teach me in the one area we had in common: the love for our children.

Because of my refusal to accept him as anything but the "Blazers killer," I knew little of his charitable work. I knew less of his love and passion for women's basketball, and how he championed its growth. I knew even less than that of the way he watched his daughters grow with unabashed love and pride, the way his eyes would sparkle whenever they laid upon any of the four. Because of my stubbornness, I failed to realize that a young man in his early twenties can be cocksure, play for the wrong team, rip your youth into shreds, make you miss school because you're too upset your team lost, and still become a forty-year-old man worth looking up to. I didn't realize that who you are in youth is barely recognizable for you as an adult.

People grow. They make mistakes, and fall, and bounce back. Not all can recover, but most do. In death, I learned that Kobe had done so—better than most—and I felt sad I missed the transition.

For the weeks that followed, I studied him more. I let myself, twenty years after "The Lob," get to know Kobe on a level many others had all those years in between, but that I had refused to do.

As a kid, I always joked with my friends that when the *I wanna be, I wanna be like Mike* jingle played in the 1990s—the one so many kids recounted in their efforts that they wanted to be just like Michael Jordan—I would alter the words to better fit my true beliefs, which was that I wanted "to be like Clyde." I was a Portlander, and a Clyde Drexler guy.

When Elle Duncan, a *SportsCenter* host on ESPN, gave an impassioned speech on Kobe and his love for his daughters, she ushered in a new moniker that traversed multiple genres. Sports and non-sports fans alike rallied around this one sentiment. The men who were in Kobe's and my shoes, fathers to daughters, had a rallying cry. For the trouble they can give us, trying, usually in vain, to understand them, there simply is nothing that compares to being—as Elle put it—a "Girl Dad."

I have three children: two girls, one boy. In my children, I found commonality with Kobe. That jingle about being "like Mike" isn't popular anymore, but if it were ever to resurface, ours would very much have been the same:

"I get to be, I get to be a Girl Dad."

And our girls would undoubtedly roll their eyes, embarrassed of our goofy dad-ness. Maybe they wouldn't appreciate it at the moment, but it wouldn't matter. Because it's about what it means overall. Growing up, shedding the skin you once wore, and evolving as a person.

I get to be a Girl Dad by raising my girls to believe in themselves during their best, as well as in their darkest times. I get to be a Girl Dad by raising my boy to know that the women in his life can do anything he can, and that he needs to treat them as equals, if not better.

I now have to raise them in a world that watched a man who loved his daughters more than anything leave us too soon.

But I get to point to that man, as well as myself, hopefully, as examples of what it means to be a Girl Dad.

We all have Kobe to thank for that; for being a shining example of fatherhood.

Introduction

The 1985 NBA Draft will go down as perhaps the deepest and most star-studded the league had (and has) ever seen. From the no-brainer, sure-fire Hall of Famers (Patrick Ewing, Karl Malone, Chris Mullin, and Joe Dumars) to the All-Stars who would prove highly valuable over their careers (Terry Porter, A. C. Green, Detlef Schrempf, Xavier McDaniel),[1] the class played an integral part in the NBA's success throughout the late 1980s and 1990s. Most of those players would go on to be foils to Michael Jordan, never getting their due thanks to his dynasty with the Chicago Bulls, but their impact was nonetheless felt.

That year's draft was also, perhaps, the most talked about for one less-than-desirable reason: the controversy that surrounded the first pick, where the New York Knicks famously won the draft

---

1   Born in West Germany, Schrempf played his college ball at the University of Washington, though would represent his home country in the 1984 and 1992 Olympics.

lottery (despite less-than-stellar odds) and drafted center Patrick Ewing from Georgetown. The circumstances around the Knicks winning the lottery still lingers in the minds of fans today. In light of past allegations of the league "fixing," or altering outcomes of games to better suit their narrative (and line their pockets with lots of money), the "frozen envelope," as the Ewing-Knicks fiasco become known, is yet another log on the fire for conspiracy theorists who view the NBA through a sequestered viewpoint.

But there was more that happened that summer than meets the eye. Specifically, more happened the day of the draft. Another subtle, yet interesting subplot, that has washed away in the hands of time, but reverberated throughout the league for the following decade.

When the Atlanta Hawks sent in their selection for the 77th pick of the draft on June 18, 1985, they did so with the understanding that their selection would be made free of controversy, and they would move on to their next pick. With future NBA players Spud Webb and Mario Elie still on the board, then Atlanta Hawks GM Stan Katsen opted to go a more untraditional route, electing to gamble on a player from Lithuania, a player the likes of which the game of basketball had never seen before. He was a mythical entity to most NBA fans in the United States, almost completely unknown to all but the most dedicated, tried-and-true basketball aficionados around the globe.

His name was Arvydas Sabonis.

He was 7-foot-3. He carried his nearly 300-pound frame like a swift, pieced-together gazelle. His court vision was unparalleled for a man his size, and his soft touch with the basketball only added to his skills. Had he been in the United States, under the guidance of a top (or even middling) program, he would have been in the running to take the number one spot from Ewing. Fortunately for the Hawks, it seemed at the time that he was too far removed off the radar despite his obvious franchise-altering potential, which jumped off the television screen just seconds into watching him play. And yet here he was, ready to be drafted far later than he should ever have been.

Bill Walton, the Hall-of-Fame center who helped guide the Trail Blazers to their lone NBA title in 1977, recalls seeing Sabonis playing overseas prior to the draft and being almost awestruck at the big man's skill set.

"He probably had a quadruple-double at halftime, and his coach, Alexander Gomelsky, didn't even start him in the second half," Walton told *Grantland* in 2011. "I said, 'You might as well just rewrite the rules of basketball after watching him play for just the first half,' the first time I ever saw him. When you think of the history of basketball, the rules were changed to make it harder for three guys: Bill Russell, Wilt Chamberlain, and Kareem Abdul-Jabbar. All the other rules have been changed to make it easier.

"He could do everything. He had the skills of Larry Bird and Pete Maravich," Walton continued. "He had the athleticism of Kareem, and he could shoot the 3-point shot. He could pass and run the floor, dribble. We should have carried out a plan in the early 1980s to kidnap him and bring him back right then."

* * *

When the Sacramento Kings selected Willie Simmons with the 76th pick, the final hurdle was removed; the Hawks were going to pair up their young star in Dominique Wilkins with their transcendent center of the future.

However, the Hawks were not the first attempt by an American outlet to lure Sabonis over. Bill Schonely, who was the long-time radio play-by-play voice of the Portland Trail Blazers, told *BlazersEdge*:

Dale Brown, who was the coach of LSU basketball [in 1985], had lost his starting center, John Williams, to the NBA draft, and Dale came up with this big idea to replace him with none other than Sabonis. Now, at the time, both President Reagan and Mikhail Gorbachev were looking for ways to build cooperation between those two Cold War foes, but coach Brown had this idea of an exchange program; an exchange program between LSU and Russia, where he would take the LSU team on a tour of the Soviet Union in return for the services of the twenty-one-year-old Arvydas Sabonis.

Now, Brown had seen Sabonis play several years before this while on a 12-game tour of the United States, and he believed him to be a Bill Walton–caliber player. Well, he ended up writing to the Soviet Union and to Gorbachev and to the White House. Well, from what I can remember about the whole situation, he actually *did* get permission to proceed, but the US government was unwilling to formally endorse this mission. So, what did coach Brown do? Brown headed to Europe himself and he tried just about everything to get Sabonis and convince him to come play. Two state department officials showed up at his door and asked that all attempts to recruit Sabonis end—and end now.

That attempt by the LSU administration aside, this was the first real attempt to lure over Sabonis. And when the Hawks made their final decision and slid the paper over to the powers that be behind the scenes of the NBA Draft, Sabonis was a Hawk.

It was perfect. Even if it took some time to bring him to America, he was theirs. Wilkins and Spud Webb on the fast break,

Sabonis tailing slightly behind, the new dominant dynasty in the East, ready to usurp the Celtics and Pistons and...

The dream was over before it could even begin.

The pick would be voided; Sabonis was underage by NBA rules, the Hawks and the NBA would later learn. The confusion came naturally, considering Sabonis had been playing professionally overseas for four years at the time, since he made his debut for BC Žalgiris in Lithuania, which played in his hometown of Kaunas.

Putting his name on the draft card not only seemed like a no-brainer, but also a legal move.

Alas . . .

"There were no rules at the time. I do know Sabonis was widely regarded as the greatest basketball player in the world at that time," said Stan Kasten, who was at the time the general manager for the Hawks, of his team's ill-fated selection.

"My guess on it was that somebody got Sabonis' birthdate wrong, and they thought he was 22, and he was not," Victor de la Serna, a journalist from Madrid, told *Vice*. "He was born in 1964, so he was only 21 [actually, Sabonis would turn 21 in December of 1985] and when the NBA found out, they voided the draft pick."

The pick, although mute, was not surprising, given the Hawks were oftentimes viewed as pioneers of early scouting in the NBA; they were the first team in the league to see the talent base growing overseas. The Hawks had selected the first- and second-ever international draftees in 1970, Mexican Manuel Raga and Italian Dino Meneghin.

"Before the whole [international] era started, we were obviously at the forefront of it," Kasten said to *Vice*. "And then the *wave* came, right after that. Just a *tremendous* wave. Try and think of the NBA today without European players in it. You can't do it."

The voiding of the Sabonis pick was crushing; not as much in the moment, since actually bringing Sabonis over was still going to be the biggest hurdle, but more for the tantalization of what he *could* be.

"I don't think any of us had especially hard feelings about it," Kasten said, "because none of us *knew* what the rules were going to be. And frankly, up until that point, we couldn't even be sure how good players were until they played in the NBA. We just didn't know. I'm sure we took it in stride. I wasn't happy about it."

Perhaps part of it was understandable. In 1985, there was no YouTube; no Internet databases to upload grainy video and study a player's tendencies, strengths, weaknesses, etc. There was the good ol' fashioned pounding of the pavement by NBA teams, sending scouts to see firsthand if the rumors about Sabonis were true.

Luckily for the Hawks (at the time), not many teams possessed the financial stability to do such things. Or, perhaps, they still viewed the travel and expenses as a waste of time and resources. With the college game in the United States thriving, why waste a scout's time traversing the landscapes in Europe, Spain, China, or anywhere outside the continental US?

But to this day, despite rampant speculation, the results of that draft night are still head-scratching at best.

Russ Granik, who was the NBA's executive vice president at the time of the draft, backs de la Serna's assertion of the fatal ambiguity being on the Hawks' end.

"I think the uncertainty about Sabonis' eligibility in 1985 had less to do with any ambiguity in the rules and related more to establishing Sabonis' age with any confidence," Granik told *Vice* through email. "We didn't have a formal relationship with FIBA at that point, so teams were kind of on their own to make sure any prospective draftees were actually eligible."

* * *

George Karl had a long and successful career coaching in the NBA, currently with the sixth-most wins in league history. He helped guide the Seattle SuperSonics (RIP) to the NBA Finals in 1996 and had helped mentor some of the brightest coaches that were under his tutelage. But before that, like many hungry up-and-comers, Karl's journey had taken him overseas to sharpen his abilities. After an unsuccessful stint with the Golden State Warriors, Karl coached the Albany Patroons for one season in the CBA before taking over Real Madrid of the Spanish League starting in 1989. His final year in 1992 netted him the job with the SuperSonics, where he inherited stars such as Gary Payton and Shawn Kemp.

But despite the successes he would go on to see, there's one piece of unfinished business that still sticks with Karl to this day.

Immediately after accepting the job in Seattle, Real Madrid signed Sabonis.

"When I came back, I was asked if I could do it all over and try again to bring a championship to Madrid, who would I try to get on my team?" Karl said to *Grantland*. "Sabonis was my answer. The best player in Europe was Sabonis. The most difficult player to play against was Sabonis. I had actually told all the NBA scouts who had come over to Europe to see Toni Kukoč and Sabonis at that time that exact the same thing. I told them 'Kukoč is good. He's an NBA player. But the best guy, if you want to win, is Sabonis.'"

By this time, six years had passed since the Atlanta Hawks' ill-fated attempt to bring Sabonis over. His career had thrived, with numerous postseason titles, lucrative contracts, and universal beliefs that he was not just the best player in Europe, but, if truth serum were in play, perhaps the world.

"People don't understand that when he was younger, Sabonis was a perimeter player and he played facing the basket," Karl continued. "He was a very athletic player, but then he tore up his Achilles in both feet, and he got bigger and thicker and wound up being more of a power player with the Trail Blazers. And one of his biggest assets was his ability to pass the ball. He could score, too, but you could run your whole offense through him, and his basketball IQ was off the charts for a 7-footer. He was always a polished player, and very few Europeans are able to step right in and have a role without spending a few years developing that role. For years, he was the best player in Europe, in my mind."

THE *(Inter)* NATIONAL
BASKETBALL
ASSOCIATION

Chapter One

THE FROZEN PICK

It was unseasonably warm in the morning of June 17, 1986, in New York City. The sun was beaming, but the temperature, admirably, topped out just in the low 80s. There was no humidity, no sweltering fumes rising from the underground. At the Felt Forum, site of that afternoon's NBA Draft, citizens strolled by, shorts and tank tops and fanny packs on, much like they do today (minus the fanny packs). Inside the Forum, the next wave of NBA stars—Dennis Rodman, Len Bias, Brad Daugherty, and Jeff Hornacek, to name a few—were just hours from entering their next phase of life, from punch-drunk college kids to millionaires overnight.

Outside, life moved on as it always did. It was New York after all, the mecca of basketball and Americana, with Broadway, cuisine, drinks, nightlife, and sex all-consuming the psyche of the passersby.

Inside, the draft that was about to take place that afternoon was facing the real possibility of falling flat compared to years past. There was no surefire, can't-miss, prodigal star on the board.

The previous few years had seen a tidal wave of superstars reinvigorate the NBA; up-and-comers like Hakeem Olajuwon, Charles Barkley, Patrick Ewing, Clyde Drexler, and Michael Jordan had dominated the summer's largest spectacle. Their appeals were already carrying over into the season, where every one of those players was establishing himself as the face of not just their respective franchise, but of the league as a whole.

But this year? In 1986? It all just felt ... flat. Daugherty, everyone rightfully predicted, was going to be a good player. A nice player. A solid player. But he wasn't Olajuwon. He wasn't Ewing. In the 1980s, big men were viewed as the be all and end all. Franchises knew that one strike of gold with a player topping seven feet could mean a decade-long run of dominance.

Armed with that rationale, the Cleveland Cavaliers selected Daugherty with the first overall pick. A nice, solid big man, capable of ... *something.* When Len Bias went second to the Boston Celtics—another big man with unlimited potential, yet zero guarantee of success—the run on forwards and guards took place.

William Bedford. Roy Tarpley. Buck Johnson. Anthony Jones.

One by one, players ticked off the board before eventually vanishing into the abyss of the NBA, gone and often forgotten.

By the time the 24th and final pick of the first round rolled around, it appeared as though another draft would end without a player being drafted straight from overseas in the initial round.

* * *

David Stern was forty-three years of age at the time, just two seasons into his reign as commissioner of the NBA. He was cocksure and a touch Napoleonic; his hair was parted strictly down the left side of his head, a linear streak of grey nestled between jet black at the break in the part, the dividing line between youth and experience.

He had called out the names of twenty-three players from colleges that sat along the Strip in Las Vegas, down to the beaches of Miami, with a multitude of stops in between. They came from the plains of Lexington, Kentucky; the contemptuous halls of Durham, North Carolina; and drop points along the eastern seaboard.

Players came and went, and with every college called out after them, it was another reminder to those watching where the true breeding grounds of the game were. The collegiate bluebloods still ruled, still fed the NBA as its de facto minor-league system. Blips here and there had come, a player dropping in from overseas here and there—usually by way of college or a thrown-in draft pick in the later rounds.

But now, a deviation.

The Portland Trail Blazers were about to make their first pick of the night, and their vice president, Bucky Buckwalter, had an ace up his sleeve.

They were going to take Arvydas Sabonis, right there and then. One year after the Atlanta Hawks had tried and failed to secure the right of Europe's biggest import, Portland was going to strike. Sabonis was legal to drink in the United States, which also meant he was (finally) able to be declared eligible by the governing bodies of the National Basketball Association.

"When I decided that we could start looking at foreign players as legitimate recruits and players in the NBA, I had some friends in Europe—primarily a player that had been at the University of Utah with me, George Fisher—who was coaching in France and then coached successfully a lot of different players, and at that time he had won two European Cups and they had played against Russia," Buckwalter tells me. "He had started talking about Arvydas Sabonis and sent me some clips. And Arvydas, at that time, was not hurt. Some of the clips that I had when Arvydas was seventeen, eighteen, nineteen years old—he was doing things that would just blow your mind. Fans here in the NBA never got to really see him because he was only playing on one leg.

"Well, I fell in love with him, then I went to see him. And then we'd decided to draft him and out of the blue I went to our owner, Larry Weinberg and I said, 'I've got this player who I think is a legitimate player and he's one of the best centers and there are people who say he's the best big man in the world. I think we should take him late in the first round. We have the 24th pick.' And he said 'Go for it.'"

The Los Angeles Lakers were picking one spot ahead, at 23, and figured to be the least likely threat to steal their big man. Although he was in the twilight of his career, the Lakers still had Kareem Abdul-Jabbar manning the middle of their attack. For this draft, at least, they were out of the center market—especially for an unknown like Sabonis.

When the Lakers selected Ken Barlow of Notre Dame, for the second time in two years Sabonis was about to hear his name selected.

But this is where things were perched on the edge, because the 24th pick still fell in the first round and what Portland was doing was unprecedented. Players born outside of the United States had been playing in the NBA for decades. Players coming directly from Europe or Africa had been suiting up in the league for more than forty years. They oftentimes found their way over through later draft picks, or via trade.

But using a first-round pick—the highest value of collateral—on a player that, while tantalizing and potentially transformative, was still such an unknown? Not only had it never been attempted before, but, for Stern, it was a slight.

The league was incubated in routine, and Stern had already gone to great lengths to ensure its rise would continue. The league was still battling its way out of the public relations nightmare that was the late-1970s and early 1980s, where rampant drug use had threatened to derail the whole operation (and, in fact, Len Bias—who went second overall to the Boston Celtics—would pass away less than two days after the draft due to a cocaine overdose). But the previous few seasons had seen the entire image flipped on its ear. Magic Johnson and Larry Bird had done their part; the Lakers-Celtics rivalry had been pure fire since those two players came into the league in 1979–80. Michael Jordan, Patrick Ewing, Clyde Drexler, and Charles Barkley were the next wave of young, talented, charismatic, marketable stars for Stern to pin his earnings on.

And what Stern was selling, wrapped up in pretty bows, was an image.

Georgetown. North Carolina. Houston. Auburn.

These players were arriving in the league with throngs of alumni on their heels, bringing eyeballs and cash to the arenas and TV screens on a nightly basis. The NBA was America and, so too were the colleges these players came from. There was no threat from the outside. Were guys like Gunther Behnke, drafted in 1985, or Eli Pasquale, drafted in 1984, welcome in the league? Of course. Were they threats to "America's Game," which basketball undoubtedly was?

No.

* * *

Stern looked pristine as he walked up to the podium to announce the Blazers' selection. He had no reason not to be; the envelope containing their pick was still sealed shut.

"For the last pick, of the first round, of the NBA Draft," Stern began. A split-second later, his face contorted, his lips slammed together in a disapproving manner. His eyes barely opened. Without raising them to engage with his audience, he offered a direct warning, a sort of State of the Union for not only his gallant beliefs, but for the NBA as a whole. After he saw Portland's draft strategy, Stern's face turned docile.

Television sets were tuned in, waiting to see if—after the previous year's blunder—Sabonis's name would be called again. With the camera set directly on his face, and all of the arrogance emanating in a clear and distinct tone, Stern began to speak.

Out of his mouth tumbled the two words that would define both his earliest egregious attitude and, also, his largest oversight into where the game of basketball—and sports in general—were heading.

"America's Game."

He shook his head slightly, the way a parent would when their child gives a bullshit story on why they ended their day in detention, then sauntered off the stage.

It was America's Game, he thought. He knew that. He believed it. He hoped.

"The Portland Trail Blazers select Arvydas Sabonis of the Soviet Union."

The fans, still sprinkled throughout the Forum, let out half-hearted chuckles. The announcers broadcasting the event on television giggled. A live shot of a draft party in Portland showed fans throwing sodas, popcorn, and anything else they could get their hands on. Some were just beside themselves. Bob Neal, who was on the television broadcast, said, "Uhh . . . well that's going to be an interesting selection," as his partner, future Hall of Famer John Thompson, put his hands on top of his head in disbelief.

But this wasn't a joke. The age limit on Sabonis had been met, finally, and it was time for foreign infiltration into the NBA to begin in earnest.

* * *

David Stern was beside himself with what had just come from his mouth. Just barely 364 days prior, the same name had been spoken, but it came in a different context than this. Sabonis's name hadn't carried the same weight in 1985; it was spoken in the fourth round, and it was for naught, as Sabonis would be found ineligible due to his age.

But now? On this night?

He knew it in his bones. Sure, many players from overseas had come through the NBA over the years. And sure, some were in the beginning stages of stardom. Some such players were spread through the college game, welcomed in from other countries, and leading their alma maters to great heights.

But what the Portland Trail Blazers were attempting to do here, in the first round, was something altogether new.

College basketball had been the NBA's own version of a minor-league affiliate for decades. The process for which it had been feeding talent to the NBA was understood, foolproof, and had yet to be truly tested by any other entity. Whether players were bred in the Midwest from the origin of the game in Indiana, sun kissed from California, hardened by the streetball pickup games of New York, or, as was becoming more and more common, traversing the Pacific or Atlantic Oceans to join a college as a way of exploring new opportunities, the NBA was a land of professionals bred from universities from all over the good ol' United States of America.

Stern believed in this system of checks and balances. With it, he could better trust the product he was showcasing for 82 games per season. He knew what he was getting from a disciple of Dean Smith. He trusted a player coming from under the wings of Larry Brown, Jerry Tarkanian, Jim Calhoun, or Bobby Knight.

Those players were tough. Disciplined. Educated in the art of rough, team-first basketball. Fans, he believed, would more easily identify with players that had been brought into their households for the previous three or four years. Players they identified from *SportsCenter* highlights.

He believed in this.

He hoped for this.

And the Blazers cared little at all.

* * *

Buckwalter wasn't amused by the arrogance in David Stern's voice when he had muttered the infamous "America's Game" drivel, but he paid little attention to it after the fact. After years of hard work, of all the paving that had been done, of all the travel and grainy footage and questions asked, Buckwalter finally, undoubtedly, had his man.

Two years prior, in the 1984 draft, Buckwalter had been a scout for the franchise when they had passed on Michael Jordan to take—you guessed it—a big man. A big man with bad ankles and horrible timing. A big man by the name of Sam Bowie, who would have a nice little career, but is now better known as the trivia answer to the most painful question you can ask a Blazers fan.[2]

But there was no imminent NBA superstar coming from college in his way now. Buckwalter had his eyes on Sabonis for years, and there were no more roadblocks in making him a Blazer.

Well, at least for the time being.

"Nobody had ever drafted any foreign players [coming straight from overseas] except in the later rounds," Buckwalter said on a

---

2   Followed by the close-second of drafting Greg Oden (a big man with bad knees) over Kevin Durant in the 2007 NBA Draft.

call with me, almost thirty-one years after that night. "There were over seven rounds, and oftentimes teams would take a throwaway pick on a foreign player."

But now the opportunity was there to smash the soft clichés into pieces. Sabonis was the antithesis of soft (another unfair label placed on players from Europe) and the furthest thing from a throwaway pick. He was a gamble of sorts—he had been playing for BC Žalgiris in Lithuania, and for the Soviet Union national team. With the turbulent relationship between the United States and the USSR—not to mention all of the internal strife that would take place between Sabonis, his native Lithuania, and the powers that be of the Soviet Premier League where they played— as much as Sabonis was an unknown to most quasi-basketball fans, his availability was just as much in question to most NBA teams looking to bring him over.

But Buckwalter and Portland were in the enviable position of being able to take a risk. Portland was coming off yet another mediocre season in 1985–86, where they went 40–42, one year after going 42–40. They weren't bad, but they weren't particularly good. Bad meant higher draft picks; good meant postseason runs and upping your street credibility for players looking for new homes. Portland possessed neither. And due to previous moves, they had already picked once in the draft, selecting Walter Berry from St. John's.

That 24th pick, though? A gift. A second chance. An opportunity to gamble a bit in hopes of striking it rich. If Sabonis was not able to make it over to the NBA, or not pan out once he did make it? No worries, they had already selected Berry.[3]

---

3   That didn't work out, either, as Berry did not want to play in Portland and would only appear in seven games before being traded to the San Antonio Spurs for Kevin Duckworth.

Regardless, it was an enviable spot for Buckwalter to be in.

"We [Portland] were a decent team, competitive in some ways, but we were always drafting in the middle of the rounds; we never got the chance to draft the top players," says Buckwalter. "We were kind of stuck in the mud."

Plus, based on where the Lakers and Celtics were in their rivalry, those two teams weren't going anywhere soon. Portland— and every other team in the league, it seemed—had time to grow and let their young rosters gel.

"When I took over, I decided we had to be innovative and do different things, so we started drafting athletes and tried to make them into basketball players. We were trying to get athletes that would be competitive with the 'Showtime' Lakers."

And Sabonis would have been just that. He was bigger, quicker, and just as—if not more-so—skilled as Kareem was for the Lakers. Along with the Celtics, the Lakers were dominating the NBA, leading them from the depths of player-led cocaine use which, in turn, drove fan disinterest and lethargy in the overall product. Magic and Larry were the faces of the league; they were as American as apple pie. Magic's smile lit up the Hollywood Strip to 10,000 volts, but he was a true midwestern boy at heart, hailing from Lansing, Michigan.

Bird was "The Hick from French Lick," Indiana, which had followed him to Boston. They were white against black, substance against style, East against West.

The Blazers, as would play out over the next six seasons, ended up being every bit as close to dethroning those two teams as anyone, but always coming up short. With Clyde Drexler, Terry Porter, Jerome Kersey, and a host of good-in-their-role players alongside them, they were a revolutionary center away from altering the course of the league's history books. When Buckwalter drafted Sabonis, he envisioned—if the big man were somehow able to make it over in the *relatively near future*—a fast-breaking, sharp-shooting, electrifying roster. Sabonis grabbed a rebound off the glass, giving precision-like outlet passes to a streaking Porter, with Drexler and Kersey flying up the sidelines.

Drexler would have been the face. Porter, the heart. Sabonis, the soul. It was all too perfect, an almost surefire recipe that could yield multiple championships . . . if all broke correctly.

And Sabonis was his baby in that project. Although far from an actual project himself, given his talents that popped when first setting eyes on him, he was still a gamble. There was the question of how he could hold up over a full NBA-length season with the travel schedule? Sabonis was used to playing between 30 and 40 games per season, with far less air travel between cities; the NBA would be eight preseason games, 82 regular season games, and potentially playoff games as well. There were the lingering questions of how his body would hold up given its massive size. There were questions of how he would be paired with Bowie, whom the Blazers had drafted two seasons prior, should the two put on the same jersey.

But, most pressing: now that he was officially part of the franchise, how would they get him over to Portland?

Bucky knew the challenges that awaited, more so after the fact of drafting him than even before. "We were committed to try and get him; he was still playing for Russia at that time, but we felt he was probably the best big man in the world that was available, so we were going to take a chance and try and get him out of the Russian orbit and into the NBA."

Oh, and it should be mentioned that, before the pick was made—before Stern had his moment of whimsical cynicism—the hoops (pardon the pun) that Buckwalter and the Blazers had already gone through to secure Sabonis were they to select him.

"I had a friend who was in Argentina at the time watching games, and I got him to ask Arvydas to meet us," Buckwalter says. "This friend spoke to Arvydas, and they set it up to where he would meet with us at 3 a.m. in the middle of the night in a room that was specially set up and vacant. It was me, Arvydas, and an interpreter. We sat and talked, and the first thing I wanted to know was if he wanted to play in the NBA, which he did. He said it had been his desire to play against the best, and we said we'd do all we could to make that happen. He said, 'I can't defect. It would be too hard on my family.' We said we'd go about it the right way, go through the state department. We did everything possible—we went directly to their federation of basketball. Russia needed money, so we offered them some, but they couldn't do it. Their bureaucracy was such that they had a hard time finding someone to make a decision. Basically, they said, 'No, not right now.'"

* * *

On top of Sabonis's obvious-to-anyone-with-eyeballs skill set, what was beginning to appeal to teams around the NBA when it came to other foreign players was the way they were being taught the game. Players weren't trying to reinvent anything or play a drastically different game; instead, they were taking the most fundamental of skills—shooting, passing, dribbling—and making it their own, and doing it ways the NBA had not seen in decades.

"In talking to the coaches, what they had done was buy films and videos of Jerry West teaching shooting, or books from coaches on the fundamentals of basketball," Buckwalter says. "European coaches were reading them and putting them in effect, and they were churning out better players year after year."

When the fundamental teachings of legendary players like West being combined with the style of play Europe was most famous for—selfless play, passing, deft shooting, court vision, and flair—the players showing up on radars around NBA offices were, well ... different than years prior. While American athletes were, on the whole, more athletic as a collective bunch, there were enough players beginning to stand out on the grainy footage that would come to America that, while executives and scouts piled on top of each other to get a glimpse of a Sabonis, other guys were starting to stand out, too.

Fortunately, they didn't have to look far. Because running alongside Sabonis on a lot of those same tapes was another player about to land on American soil, for the same franchise that was hedging its bets on the big man.

And because of that, later that June 17 afternoon, shortly after Sabonis's name was called, Dražen Petrović heard his name, too.

* * *

Portland selected Petrović in the third round with the 60th overall pick, 36 slots after Sabonis. The two players had known each other for years, having played against one another on numerous occasions. The thought of those two running alongside each other for the same franchise enticed Buckwalter. However, like Sabonis, Petrović was not a lock to make it to America anytime soon.

But what scouts saw on tape—a 6-foot-5 version "Pistol Pete" Maravich, as some scouts compared him to—made the gamble acceptable. What Sabonis, and specifically, Petrović, had in spades was an unyielding desire to compete and be the best player in the world.

"In addition to drafting athletes and hoping to turn them into basketball players, we thought there might be foreign players who could compete," says Buckwalter. "Most coaches and people I talked to at that time scoffed at the idea that any foreign players were good enough to play in the NBA. I had seen Arvydas Sabonis and Dražen Petrović on film quite a bit, then when Arvydas toured the United States I met [with] him a little bit and became very interested in him."

The traveling tours Sabonis, Petrović, and other players looking to make a name for themselves in the states went on were instrumental in receiving the type of attention necessary for an NBA team to take a shot.

"He [Sabonis] was playing in an All-Star Game in Madrid, Spain [after the 1986 draft], so I went over to Spain," says Buckwalter. "He had known we drafted him, yet it was hard to get to him because his team in Russia was very protective. They would literally tuck the players into bed at night [after games]. We didn't get to interact with him at all."

That type of miscommunication, misinformation, and child-like behavior was commonplace in the 1980s. Tensions around the globe were escalated, as leaders from major countries sought ownership of nearly everything. Whether it was religion, money, oil, or, as was becoming more evident, sports, nothing was off the table. So, if Buckwalter and the Blazers wanted Sabonis, they realized they may literally have to untuck him from the bed that he was lying in, in order to show him there were true opportunities in the Western world.

* * *

By 1988, two years after being drafted together by the Blazers, neither Sabonis nor Petrović had made their way stateside. When the Olympics began that summer in Seoul, South Korea, Buckwalter made it a point to locate the two players to assess and get an honest view of their relationship; to see if they meshed together and to try, maybe, to see if the NBA was in their near futures. If he had any hope at getting one player to defect, odds were better if he could get both on the same page—a pure package deal.

The trick would be getting the two men in the same room. Sabonis, along with future basketball Hall of Famer Šarūnas Marčiulionis, was starting for the Soviet Union, and would take home the gold medal in the final Olympics before the United States was allowed to send professional players.

Petrović, playing for the Yugoslavian national team alongside Vlade Divac and Toni Kukoč, took home the silver medal. And due to the odd relationship among Eastern European intersquads, it seemed like a million-to-one shot that Buckwalter would be able to get both of his players in one room, let alone to chat.

As it turns out, it would be easier than he thought—on all accounts. The Soviet Union and Yugoslavian teams would square off in the opening round on Sunday, September 18, 1988, with Petrović—and his 25 points—leading an upset victory, in which Sabonis was held to just 11 points.

Then, on September 30, the two teams would square off again in the title game. This time, Sabonis would prove to be an unstoppable force, notching 20 points, 15 rebounds, and 3 blocks, securing the gold medal in a 76–63 victory. Petrović, for his part, was again masterful, scoring 24 points, though it wouldn't be enough.

But this, Buckwalter knew, was his shot. The two men, in the same arena—and, perhaps most importantly—with the same postgame affairs to attend to. As in Olympics protocol, after every title game, players are required to submit a urine sample to test for any illicit drugs or steroids. The testing would take place in a single room, where players would file in and out, one by one, until the monotonous deed was over.

It was time. And, as it turned out, was almost too easy.

"Sabonis was healthy enough to play in the 1988 Olympics. In one of the games, he went up against Dražen. There was a big media build-up in Europe about who was the best player. Dražen was considered to be the best shooting guard, and Sabonis was considered to be the best big man, and we had drafted both of them. The issue was everyone was saying there was no way they'd ever play together because of the rivalry [of their countries]. After the game where Russia won the championship, they went in to have their specimen checked—which was required after the Olympic competition—and Dražen said, 'I can't do it. I need a beer, maybe it will help me.' He got a beer, and the dressing room was close to Sabonis's, and he said, 'Well, I'd like a beer, too,' so they sat down and had a beer in the same place. After that they came out, I was standing there waiting for them. They came out, arm in arm, and I thought, *Oh my God, look at that. Wouldn't that be nice to have.*

The pipe dream appeared to be coming into focus. Perhaps a friendship was in the works; perhaps the pull of America, the NBA, and the millions of dollars that awaited them would be the final nudge needed to bring the two most tantalizing imports to the United States.

The performance that Petrović put on the following June during the 1989 European Championship tournament only enhanced what the Blazers believed they would be getting.

As Todd Spehr wrote in his biography of Petrović, *The Mozart of Basketball*:

There was something electric and everlasting about the way Petrović played in that 1989 European Championship tournament. For years he had been a brilliant individual star, but the national team had seemed in varying ways to come up short, a talented team that failed to make the pieces fit. Finally, there seems to be a correlation between Petrović's greatness and that of the team. His tournament numbers seem exaggerated: 30 points per game, 69 percent shooting from the field on mostly perimeter shots, the average winning margin of his team at 22 points.

But the numbers weren't exaggerated; they were very much real, just as the legendary status he was beginning to build. Petrović's path to stardom was being paved by his own talents and perseverance, and that drive had been forged in the fires of the real world, one that sports often leaves behind.

* * *

In 2010, as part of their *30 for 30* collection, ESPN released *Once Brothers*, a comprehensive and emotional breakdown of international basketball relations—mainly, between NBA greats Vlade Divac and Dražen Petrović—and how their friendship (and eventual turmoil) shaped the Yugoslavian national team. Watch it once, however, and the legend of Petrović comes further into light.

In it, you get a sense of who Petrović was as both a man and a player, and the drive he carried with him to perform at his very best.

"Dražen was a killer," Dino Rađa, who played alongside Petrović for the Yugoslavian national team starting in 1987, and later for the Boston Celtics, said Spehr in his book. "He was the only man I know who could beat himself."

As would play out over the coming decades, as more and more players headed west to play in the NBA, Petrović carried a unique—and somewhat heartwarming—confidence. It's a product of the culture he was born into, as is so often the case with the best of the best. Whether through a perceived slight at the behest of their peers or an unwavering desire to outshine anyone in their path, what separates the good from the great, and then again the elite from that group, is the desire to find the extra one percent that no one else is capable of reaching.

For some, it's an extra level of work ethic. For others, it's outfitting your game with additional tools that are deemed impossible to stop. Still, for others, it's simply a combination of the two And for Petrović, he was blessed with the ability to channel those: the extra drive, the skills, and the mind to outwit anyone he went up against.

It also helped that the way he was taught to play the game, and the environment in which he was brought up, only aided in his development.

The game of basketball was taught to Petrović with a level of panache. The crowds that attend games where he played in his developmental years came armed with the same feeling. Whereas in the United States the home fans come, sit in their seats with overpriced hot dogs and beer, and cheer when their team does well—or when prompted by the public address announcer—fans in other countries make it an *experience*. It's entertainment, not life or death (unless you locate yourself in certain areas where fútbol is king; in that case, all bets are off).

The games being played in gymnasiums around the globe are more than that; they're parties filled with bands, flags, banners ... you name it, patrons have them. They're not in their seats; that's where their coats lie. People stand and dance and sing like their nightly entertainment depends on it. When players arrive in America, they're immersed in a much different atmosphere, but their upbringings still shine through. They talk to fans and to other players. They smile and laugh and are gregarious.

"Dražen could talk trash in four languages," Reggie Miller, the Royal Highness of trash talk himself, would say years later after he had faced Petrović.

But his skills went far beyond the dribble that came from his lips.

"To his fellow Yugoslavs, Dražen Petrović was Michael/Magic/Larry all wrapped up in one," noted author Jack McCallum once wrote for *Sports Illustrated*. "He was the player who had lifted Yugoslavia to international basketball prominence, like Magic and Larry; he was the most talented and showiest player, like Michael; and he was the most competitive, go-for-the-jugular player, like all three of them."

* * *

To get to that point, Petrović had taken a wide path full of twists and turns. After a year in the military, Dražen had joined his older brother, Aleksandar, on the KK Cibona team. The first year in Cibona he won both the Yugoslav championship and the National Cup. In 1985, Petrović had a performance that seems to be some sort of mythical story or tall tale. In a game against Slovenian team KK Union Olimpija, Petrović scored 112 points.

"How we train here at the Basketball Club Zagreb, we do not do specialization. When a player starts to train with us, he will learn to play all positions," said Andrej Tesla, who coached Dražen for KK Zagreb in Croatia. "Dražen Petrović has a special place in Croatian basketball history. Not to say that people such as Toni Kukoč, Dino Rađa, none of those people are unimportant in any way ... they're all important, they're all pieces of the puzzle that made Croatian basketball what it is."

He averaged 37.7 points in his four years with Cibona and was the Croatian Player of the Year all four seasons.

"He was one of the first guys to shoot from three- and four-feet behind the line, and he was doing it running full speed off screens," says Rick Carlisle, who was an assistant with the Nets during Petrović's two-plus seasons there. "It was absolutely wild. He would be perfectly suited to play today. From the standpoint of work ethic and getting better, I put him in [Dirk] Nowitzki's class."

Petrović hit 43.7 percent of his career 3s, the fifth-best mark in league history. Every Croatian with any connection to basketball seems to know that statistic by heart.

"When he missed an open 3, you couldn't believe it," says Willis Reed, the Nets' GM at the time. "He was money."

After one lunch during training camp, Danny Ainge and Petrović, teammates on the Portland Trail Blazers, retired to Petrović's apartment to hang out between two-a-day practices. Ainge plopped into a bean bag chair and fell asleep. He woke up to Petrović pedaling an exercise bike at full speed. "He was just so driven," Ainge says. "Not playing bothered him more than anyone I ever met."

"Dražen was one of the greatest players ever," Slovenian NBA player Rasho Nesterović told *Bleacher Report* in 2012. "Back home, 90 percent of kids tried to be like him. His hard work inspired a lot of kids. Dražen and I were very good friends. I was one of those people who welcomed him to Portland when he came from Europe. We talked about his family a lot in his restaurant, and he enjoyed his friends and he enjoyed the game of basketball. I really respect him because he worked very, very hard.

"Dražen Petrović was an extraordinary young man, and a true pioneer in the global sports of basketball," NBA commissioner David Stern once said of Petrović's importance to the NBA. "I know that a lasting part of his athletic legacy will be that he paved the way for other international players to compete successfully in the NBA. His contributions to the sport of basketball were enormous. We are all proud of the fact we knew him."

What he could have been—truly been—was something fans, family, and Dražen himself were robbed of seeing. Although Petrović would make his NBA debut for the Blazers in 1989, the franchise and player would prove to be an odd fit. With Drexler blossoming into the one the game's 50 Greatest Players, the role Petrović was best suited for—flashy, ball-in-hand playmaker and distributor—never came to fruition. He was a solid player off the bench, but never more.

"I really respect him because he worked very, very hard," said Clyde Drexler, who teamed with Petrović during his tenure in Portland, and—because of the position they each played—is perhaps most responsible for him not seeing the playing time he deserved. "Each and every day in practice he would be the first guy to come and the last guy to leave the gym. So anybody with that kind of dedication ... you have to have a lot of respect for him."

A fresh start came when he was traded to the New Jersey Nets during the 1990–91 season. After averaging just 4.4 points per game over 7.4 minutes per game in his final season in Portland, the move to New Jersey would be a reawakening for one of the game's potential stars.[4]

Over three seasons with the Nets, he would see his minutes-per-game skyrocket to 20.5, then 36.9, and finally 38. His points-per-game followed suit, from 12.6 to 20.6 to 22.3, the latter of which while shooting 45 percent from three-point range.

---

4   In 95 games for the Blazers, Petrović never started and played 30 minutes or more twice.

Then, tragedy.

Petrović would lose his life in a car accident on June 7, 1993. He was twenty-eight years old, and on the brink of becoming the next true international superstar, alongside Vlade Divac. Although he had years remaining to keep making an impact across the globe, Petrović is still regarded as one of the biggest influences on kids growing up in Europe and around the globe almost thirty years later.

"When he [Petrović] got in the league as young as he was, and he started scoring 40 points, 50 points, he was by himself," jokes Toni Kukoč. "He was all about basketball. I would joke with him 'Do you know anything else? Do you know anything about music, or anything else that's not basketball?'

"As much as you want to talk about Croatian basketball, it's impossible to not mention Dražen's name."

Even players today, nearly three decades after his passing, know well the legend of Dražen.

"He was the guy who helped win the last medal for Croatian national team, was our most popular athlete and probably the best," forward Bojan Bogdanović told *The Athletic* in 2018. "Everyone knew who he was and why. He was one of the first European players in the NBA, so he opened the doors to the NBA for Europeans, not just Croatians. You looked up to that and respected it."

Chapter Two

WHERE IT BEGAN

"It was only fitting that one of the very first NBA international teams won its first-ever championship on the road by a squad with unwanted players who played a game that was created by a man [James Naismith] who was born in Canada."

—Daniel Kucin Jr., the *Sentinel* newspapers, July 9, 2019

The Basketball Association of America (BAA) was founded in 1946, the byproduct of owners of the major ice hockey arenas in the northeastern and midwestern United States and Canada. And so, it was that, on November 1, 1946, in Toronto, Canada, the Toronto Huskies played host to the New York Knickerbockers at Maple Leaf Gardens. Though there were similar attempts in years prior—the American Basketball League and National Basketball League had attempted to get off the ground in decades prior, with little to no success—this game, by historians, is most often referred to as the first-ever professional basketball game. What helped the BAA's cause was that the league was the first to attempt to play primarily in large arenas, in major cities, around the country.

Although the leagues would only be known as the BAA for a short time, before a series of mergers morphed into the National Basketball Association that we know today, its impact was massive. Most of the players that came and went during that short period have been lost in the history books, but one man, Henry Biasatti, made a lasting impact.

Henry Biasatti was born in the Kingdom of Italy on January 14, 1922. Twenty-four years later, in 1946, he would become the first international player to play professional basketball in the United States of America. Biasatti suited up for the Toronto Huskies, who lost that opening night to the Knickerbockers, 68–66. The game itself is noteworthy for the legacy it began, and the impact that its final NBA product has made. But for the direction the game is going, with more and more foreign players rising to the top of the NBA ranks, it was Biasatti's presence—perhaps more than any other individual player—which left the largest imprint. Although it would be almost five full decades before players of his ilk were the norm in the league, the ice had to be broken at some point. The international stars of today have Henry Biasatti to thank for that.

While the San Antonio Spurs seemingly claim the non-trade-marked title of the NBA's most Euro-influenced franchise, the Denver Nuggets began to nip at their heels as the aughts rolled along. With stars such as Nikola Jokić, Danilo Gallinari, and the since-departed Jusuf Nurkić, the Nuggets have turned into the latest feeding ground for European stars. Since 2011, in fact, the Nuggets have acquired 11 players born overseas. Cultural hierarchy has played a role in Denver's success, as the city's population has a diverse heritage breakdown; in 2019, German (14.6 percent), Irish (9.7 percent), and Italian (4.0 percent) made up almost 30 percent of the census.

While franchises such as the Spurs and Nuggets have benefitted from their demographics, they've also been at the forefront of scouring the Euro leagues for talent.

"I don't think it matters where a guy plays," Joshua Riddell, a scout for *DraftExpress*, said in 2016. "You can basically see anyone on Synergy [a scouting service with a database of league games from around the world] a few hours after their game ends."

"Your list of contacts in each region has to be profound because players nowadays are coming from anywhere," former Nuggets GM Artūras Karnišovas said. "You have to know people, from coaches to GMs to agents. You have to be familiar with all the layers."

According to Jonathan Tjarks of *The Ringer*:

The biggest advantage the Nuggets have is the familiarity of their front office with the international game. Connelly was a longtime international scout, and Karnišovas [now GM of the Chicago Bulls] was one of the greatest players in European history before starting a career in management. They still travel overseas regularly, but their man on the ground in Europe these days is Rafal Juc, a 24-year-old from Poland who has quickly made a name for himself in the industry.

"Rafal is the most popular man in Europe. He's really well connected around the continent," Elan Vinokurov, the president and owner of EV Hoops, a scouting and consulting service used by multiple NBA teams, told Tjarks in 2016. "He has established himself at a young age. When he talks about a player, you sit up and take notice."

"Friends often tell me that you get paid to watch basketball, that's not really a job," Vinokurov continued. "However, I bet some people that think it's a dream wouldn't last very long doing it. You have to be passionately in love with basketball because you are watching thousands of games a year, most of them far below the NBA level. It's not a 9-to-5. You have to be available 24/7. When I am home, I am watching at least two games a day, and I'm always networking with coaches, agents, and players and my colleagues back in the U.S.

"A more experienced scout told me that when you are on time with a player, you are late," Juc told Tjarks. "You have to look at the big picture when evaluating an international player. Not only the player, but his coach, opposition, and teammates should be scouted too. That's why some teams still do not feel comfortable scouting Europeans."

The developmental path in Europe is a lot more varied than in the United States. Players go pro at different ages, they compete in different leagues across the continent with different basketball cultures and levels of play, and they have wildly different roles on their respective teams.

"Probably the biggest challenge is assessing the competition and seeing these guys play against other potential NBA players," Riddell says. "You'll see Kentucky or Duke players matched up against other draft hopefuls all year round in meaningful games to provide some context for how they look compared to their peers. International players are all spread out and don't get the same type of exposure in professional games where their coaches have more pressure to win."

As Evan Daniels of FOX Sports wrote in January 2017, the trickle-down effect can be felt at the collegiate level, too: "According to a study done by Rukkus Blog on 2016–2017 rosters, 11 percent of college basketball players are born outside of the United States. The total number of foreign-born prospects on college rosters is up 40 percent in the last 10 years."

David Patrick, an assistant coach for the TCU basketball team, told FOX Sports, "there's been a significant increase in coaches attempting to do what he and Gonzaga assistant Tommy Lloyd, who has built a strong reputation with his international contacts, seemingly have mastered."

"Me in Australia and even Tommy [Lloyd] in Europe could probably call our connections and someone could tell me over the phone who was good enough," Patrick continued. "Then I would do the legwork and go over there.

"When I used to do that, there were probably only two or three schools that would be there," he added. "You're talking seven years ago. Now I went over in July to Australia and there were 50 schools there in a two-day period."

Playing in the United States for college brings increased exposure to the public via television, but also to NBA scouts who scour college games and practices during the season.

"Ben Simmons, for example, he had an opportunity to make seven figures playing overseas last year," Patrick said. "But he understood the importance if he came to college, the marketing, and how much he would be marketed if he was on FOX and ESPN night in and night out."

NBA Draft expert Jonathan Givony of *DraftExpress* told FOX Sports that the college exposure certainly helped [Jakob] Pöltl and [Domantas] Sabonis become lottery picks in the 2016 draft.

"They wouldn't have been first-rounders if they hadn't played college basketball," Givony said. "Guys are seeing the success Sabonis and Pöltl had and they are thinking, 'Why can't it be me?'"

Despite the advancements in technology, which have flipped the script on scouting overseas, Mark Titus of *Grantland* came away from his time in the trenches with one underlying feeling. "Of all the things I learned at Pro Scout School, one thing stood out: Being an NBA scout is probably the single worst job in the world."

"Tony Ronzone [a scout for the Dallas Mavericks at the time], who has experience as an international scout, provided my favorite moment of the entire two days when he recalled how he scouted a 7-foot-9 North Korean player named Michael Ri. Ronzone met face to face with Kim Jong-il and negotiated a 'wheat deal' to bring Ri to the NBA," wrote Titus. "Apparently, the Dear Leader told Ronzone he would allow Ri to leave North Korea and play professional basketball if the team paid Kim's regime in wheat. Ronzone added that he's missed a lot of flights in his life but made absolutely certain he didn't miss the one out of North Korea because 'there are only two flights out of the country—Tuesday and Friday.'"

As Sam Hinkie told *Grantland* in a 2011 interview—long before he became attached at the hip with "The Process" as GM of the Sixers—the scouting process goes deeper than access and eyes. "Our scouting staff in Houston [with the Rockets] works incredibly hard scouring the globe for talent. Everyone is constantly on the lookout for differential information that might yield additional predictive power to our player evaluations. No doubt, predictive power is what we're all after. And data helps. But information with real power comes in a variety of forms: both in the stereotypical form that the movie will surely play up of databases and spreadsheets and analysts and predictive models, *but also* in the form of expertise and experience acquired only via a lifetime of playing and coaching the game. The best organizations bring that all together."

* * *

In 1995, nearly ten years after the Blazers originally drafted him, Sabonis was ready to make his NBA debut.

He met with Bob Whitsitt, then the Blazers' general manager, over dinner in Spain. The surreal nature of the meeting wasn't lost on anyone; Spain, after all, is where Sabonis had originally met Bucky Buckwalter all those years ago, under the cover of night, in a dark hotel. Sabonis then was a man without options.

Now, he was free.

"[Whitsitt] said if I don't come now, I wouldn't get to come ever, that I wouldn't get to feel what is the NBA," Sabonis told *Grantland*. "It was the last bullet, you know? I decided I'm 30 years old, and Portland called me and said if you want, let's go, and I finished the contract with Real Madrid, and if I didn't come now, I didn't come ever; I don't get to feel what is NBA," Sabonis said. "It was the last bullet, you know?"

What the NBA would be getting, though, was a shell of the man who had terrorized leagues around the world for almost 14 years. Bob Cook, the Blazers' team doctor at the time, said Sabonis could "qualify for a handicapped parking spot based on the X-rays alone" of his feet and ankles. The wear and tear of the 7-foot-3, 300-pounder was hindering his performance; it wasn't if, but when, that it would be the final downfall for the Lithuanian.

"When we were bringing him over [from Europe], Bob put me in charge of getting Arvydas and his family set up in Portland, in every aspect," Jim Paxson told Kerry Eggers for his book *Jail Blazers*. "We developed a close relationship. He would invite me to dinner when he had family in from out of town.

"As a player, even though limited physically by the time he got to America, I believe he's a top-20 player in the history of the game. His ability to pass, to shoot, to do all of the things big men in today's game—he was doing all of those things in the late 1980's and 90's. When we had him [from 1995 to 2003], he didn't have the athleticism anymore, but he had a great feel for the game, and he really cared about winning."

Outside of some run-ins with teammate Rasheed Wallace—himself a temperamental and hot-headed wild card—Sabonis was adored by fans, teammates, and media alike, all of whom absorbed the baritone-voiced behemoth for his cultural differences and quirks.

"I loved coaching Arvydas. He was nowhere near physically what he had been before his leg problems," P. J. Carlesimo, who coached Sabonis in Portland, told Eggers. "But with us, the skill level was still very good, the way to be shot and passed. He didn't stop [Shaquille O'Neal], but we more than anybody could play him one-on-one. Shaq couldn't move Sabonis like he could the other guys. Nobody could play Shaq physically the way Arvydas could. He was an unbelievable passer. It was hard for him to do 82 games, but he was one of my favorite players I ever coached."

Chapter Three

GOT ANY CHANGE
(IN YOUR STYLE OF PLAY)?

"You either have an eye for talent or you don't. You can do all
your homework and have everything properly organized, but
when it's draft night and you're on the clock and your coconuts
are on the table—when it's nut-cutting time, as we say—that's
when you separate the boys from the men."

—Donnie Nelson, *Grantland*, 2012

According to longtime GM and scout Donnie Nelson, the NBA
over the 1980s and 1990s had been either a direct hit or a wild,
miscalculated miss in their exploration of international talent.
Certain players like Dirk Nowitzki, Steve Nash—who is Canadian, but went to college in the United States, yet did not receive
much attention coming out of high school—Peja Stojaković,
and others had catapulted onto the scene during the mid-to-
late 1990s, showing that identifying true difference makers from
overseas was more of a crapshoot than it was for players who had
spent more time in America. But those players—the impactful
ones that leave marks on the game—were not coming along
often. True enough, until late in the 2000s, very few teams even
employed full-time international scouts; too often, the notion of

drafting players from overseas was viewed as a part-time venture, despite the growing number of players who were beginning to become household names in the States.

For many franchises around the NBA—especially those in smaller, more cash-strapped markets—putting too much effort into overseas scouting felt like a thinning out of precious resources. Unlike the NFL or top-tier conferences such as the Big Ten, SEC, or ACC in collegiate sports, there are no $20 billion TV contracts for teams to sponge off in the NBA, flooding their departments with larger staffs. By and large, franchises are at the whim of their owners; the stingier the owner, the stingier the product on the floor.

Until the not-so-distant past, overseas scouting still came with stipulations of second-hand information and gut-instinct intuition. Until the early 2010s, there was no YouTube or online scouting services such as EV Hoops to log onto when you wanted to watch film of a particular league or player. More often than not, teams were left trying to dissect a player's ability while watching them play against inferior competition, or against players twice—or sometimes half, depending on the league—their age, on grainy video. It was still a process that came straight from a cheesy sports-movie montage: small, cramped offices with lowly paid, overworked scouts, cigarettes in hand, fast food bags strung about, as they pored over the grainy film, coffee-stained scouting reports fed in from Helsinki, Granada, or Spain all over their desks. And the perception of the players that came over—unfair, but real—was lagging behind the times.

As Bill Simmons, famed creator of *Grantland* and *The Ringer*, told *Deadspin* in 2017, "I'm very xenophobic when it comes to the NBA draft—too many foreign guys have bombed miserably, everyone underestimates the cultural adjustment ... We overrate the younger foreigners, even though they're playing against crappy competition . . . I don't get it. What a screwed-up league."

But while the scouting had taken time to evolve, the players who were given their opportunity to shine had wasted no time. Once certain players began to climb to the top of the NBA mountain, it became clear that—for the most part—the perception that players who were coming straight from overseas weren't ready for the rigors of the NBA weren't true.

"There was an overreaction during those years [the late 1990s]," says Nelson. "We went from having no emphasis on international players, to the '90s when we had the 'Jackie Robinson' years, to bringing in [Pau] Gasol and [Dirk] Nowitzki and [Tony] Parker and those guys, and then all of a sudden it went too far."

Nelson gave that quote in 2012, for an article titled "Is the NBA Done Drafting International Players?" for *Grantland*. In the years after that article was published, some of the game's biggest stars—Giannis Antetokounmpo, Luka Dončić, Kristaps Porziņģis—would be drafted high in the first round, straight from professional leagues around the globe, and have proven to be perennial MVP candidates. Giannis, in fact, already has one to his name.

That particular article came after a woeful 2012 NBA Draft, in which nine international players were taken. One, Evan Fournier, carved out a semi-respectable NBA career; the other eight combined made less than a blip on the radar. At the time, it seemed like a completely valid question to ask, but it also showed the vulnerability in which international players still carried.

In every draft there are countless American-born players, or players from other countries that came to America and played college ball, who flame out in the league. It's apparent that there is no movement toward not selecting those players. That type of thinking, however, still shows the negative connotation that players with no Americanized backgrounds carry, even after now decades of proof otherwise. As proof, in the 2012 NBA Draft, of the 60 players drafted (not including the nine players noted above), 23 played no more than four years in the league.

Oftentimes, the scouting of international talent was diced up and bungled due to the egos of those involved. In an effort to prove themselves as the smartest man in the room, scouts would often talk themselves into—or out of—a particular player when, in reality, all they had to do was take a look to their left and right in the stands. If they did, they would see barren land and know that it wasn't a battle of scout on scout anymore, where one man was trying to be smarter than the other. It was simply them watching and studying the player on the floor, showcasing their skills.

"In the '90s, you could go to a major European game, with tons of NBA-ready players, and not see a single NBA scout in the building," Rich Sheubrooks, who was an executive director of global and pro scouting for the Utah Jazz, told *Grantland* in 2012. "And then in the early 2000s, you'd show up to a game somewhere obscure like Austria, and there are six NBA guys in there watching."

In 1989—three years after the drafting of Arvydas Sabonis and Dražen Petrović—the Los Angeles Lakers, finally in need of a center to replace Kareem Abdul-Jabbar, selected Vlade Divac with the 26th pick of the first round. Divac, who had played professionally in Yugoslavia for KK Sloga, was just twenty-one years old, but already a seasoned vet in the professional ranks.

At just fourteen years of age, Divac had left his hometown of Prijepolje, Serbia. The war-torn nation, which had been under constant distress for more than a century, offered little to Vlade and his family in the long run. Even at an early age, it became clear that the child was bred for something special in the game of basketball, and his calling lied outside his homeland. Although he began his career shortly after for KK Elan near Prijepolje, it wasn't long before he was off to Yugoslavia to play for KK Sloga, where he made waves by scoring 27 points in a game. A game, as you can imagine, against grown men, some of which were nearly three-times his age.

For Divac, the growing pains—and being removed from his parents—was both a trial and an ultimate life lesson.

"When those things happen, you go back in your career and where you came from, and I remember the details when I made a big decision for myself and for my family basically," Divac told NBC Sports in 2019. "I was just 14 years [old], and I had to leave my parents to pursue basketball."

By the time the 1989 season rolled around, Divac, then twenty-one, was ready to make the leap to the United States. Unlike Sabonis, who topped the scales at 300 pounds, Divac played the game like a vision into the future of the NBA, when centers were more sinewy, rather than bulky, and possessed a skill set beyond just the ability to back a player down and overpower them.

Divac would make an immediate impact for the Lakers; he was selected for the NBA's All-Rookie Team despite splitting his time behind Abdul-Jabbar and still learning the English language.

"The Lakers were a perfect fit for me, with Dr. [Jerry] Buss, with Jerry West, with Magic, Byron Scott, James Worthy, Pat Riley—they all had a part of helping me adjust to U.S. life and NBA style," Divac continued.

West, one of the most influential figures in NBA history, is another visionary in terms of his ability to assess talent and look beyond the surroundings of an individual.

"At that point in time, not many people had as much confidence in European players as they do today," West said in the ESPN *30 for 30* documentary *Once Brothers*. "And so, he fell to us late in the draft, and even though we'd never seen him play in person, we said, what the heck?"

That gamble was never lost on Divac.

"He is a guy that kind of bet on me," Divac says of West. "When I came to New York for the draft in '89, they told me I should be [picked] like 10 and 15, and it didn't happen. So, I was very disappointed, like, nobody wants me. But Jerry had picked 26, so he picked me. Later on, I figured out that if I chose a team, probably, I would have made a mistake."

Once Divac arrived in Tinseltown, and started to make a name for himself in the NBA circles with his passing skills and soft touch around the rim—as well as his ability to deftly mesh with the core of Johnson, Worthy, and Abdul-Jabbar—his returns to Serbia and the Yugoslavian national teams took on even more weight. When paired up again with Petrović for summer tournaments and the Olympics, they thrived.

"My generation started in big tournaments," Divac said. "[The] '88 Olympics, we got silver. [The] '89 European Championship, we got gold. In the 1990 World Cup in Argentina, we got gold. [The] '91 European Championship, we got gold, and then there was a civil war, and for three years, we didn't play."

After Petrović's death in 1993, Divac was the leader of the NBA's European movement. Alongside Toni Kukoč—who took a comfortable seat on the Chicago Bulls' dynasty bus—and Dino Rađa of the Boston Celtics by way of Croatia (who played with Divac on the storied pre-Civil War Yugoslavian national team), the trio was painting a new picture for the future of the league as it pertained to international players.

"A few years before, there were a few Europeans that came for a month [to the NBA] and came back, but when I finally made it, I was so proud that we kind of opened the door for internationals," Divac said.

"There were foreign players before him, but a lot of players that came over struggled, and Vlade paved the way for a lot of guys to follow him," Scot Pollard, who teamed with Vlade in Sacramento, told NBC Sports. "Whether they give him credit or not, they really should. He was a trailblazer for the European players to come over."

Even fifteen years after his retirement, Divac is looked upon as a cult hero among both NBA fans—who revered his style of play and carefree attitude—as well as the new generation of players who have come up under his shadow.

"He is one of our first icebreakers that come over from Europe," Serbian-born wing Bojan Bogdanović told NBC Sports California recently. "He led the way for a lot of European athletes to come overseas and play in the NBA. He's one of the greatest players to ever play."

Divac is now with the Sacramento Kings, the franchise that he helped put on the map. During his time with the Kings, from 2000 to 2003, the franchise took on a new life-form, transforming from a once dormant, almost nonexistent entity to arguably the league's most exciting brand. Alongside Jason Williams—a.k.a. "White Chocolate"—Chris Webber, (Croatian-born) Peja Stojaković, and a host of perfectly fitting role players, the Kings were known for slugging it out and, some would argue, being cheated out of winning the Western Conference finals in 2002, when the Lakers stole a victory in Game Seven, on the way to winning their third straight NBA championship. And although his career would continue on before announcing his retirement in 2005, it was Divac's time in Sacramento that helped ignite the flames of the European movement once again.

While he was inducted into the Basketball Hall of Fame in 2019 for his on-court accomplishments, Divac is known as much around the world for his off-court philanthropic efforts, as well as for the impact he has had on the globalization of the game.

"It's just a testament to a guy who has handled himself as a player and of course, going forward from there as an executive, in a very classy way," former Kings coach Dave Joerger told NBC Sports. "He's a guy that everyone wants to be around."

Divac looks back on those times when it all seemed too expansive—the fourteen-year-old boy setting out on his own accord to preserve a life for him and his family—and sees the way it shaped now only his life, but those who came in behind him.

* * *

Divac's impact on the court is as visible today as it's ever been. From 2001 to 2009, the NBA went through an offensively challenged period. For instance, in the 2000–01 season, teams averaged just 94.8 points per game; at the time, that was the lowest since the 1954–55 season (the first season using the shot clock). It bottomed out in 2004, when the average dipped to 93.4 points. It was a combination of style (teams still preferred to use the traditional center with his back to the basket, one-on-one style of play) and a declining lack of skill among the big men who were tasked with playing that way.

However, thanks in part to players like Sabonis, Divac, Hakeem Olajuwon (who played at the University of Houston), and Dirk Nowitzki, the perception of European—and international—big men has changed dramatically since. The ramifications of the way those men played the game, with skill, and size—almost like 7-foot point guards—the game has altered dramatically. In the 2019–20 season, the league-wide scoring average was 111.4, the highest since the 1969–70 season.

Although there is no direct correlation to those players (and certainly lots of factors have come into play, such as coaching philosophies, rule changes, and an ever-evolving skill group of players), it's not hard to see the impact players like Divac had.

"I have to give a lot of credit to David Stern to open up the league, but also in my case, Jerry West and Dr. Buss that had the vision of international guys making it to the NBA," Divac said. "And now, watching the NBA, it's the most popular league in the world just because we have more than 30 percent international guys in the league."

Sometimes, though, it takes a player who was just down the bench to recognize the true talents and influence one player brings.

"I think European players before Vlade, most of them struggled because they were trying to play the way they were [coached], but then they were trying to adapt more to the NBA style," Pollard said. "Whereas Vlade was like, 'I'm just going to keep playing the way I play,' and his style ended up, I think, altering the game, and that's why I think he belongs in the Hall of Fame.

"Vlade brought a different style to the NBA, and it stuck."

* * *

Perhaps no other player personified and revolutionized that change in style more than Dirk Nowitzki. The NBA's all-time foreign-born scoring leader (and sixth overall, with 31,560 points—just behind Michael Jordan's 32,292), Dirk's introduction to the NBA and its fans came about in a more direct way than others who had attempted to make the NBA jump before him. Having to navigate through multiple hoops (pun intended) to make it—including funneling through the AAU circuit—Nowitzki found himself at the Alamo Stadium Gymnasium in San Antonio, Texas, in the spring of 1998 to play in the Nike Hoop Summit.

Nowitzki was invited to the Summit as part of the World Team, which featured future NBA players such as Argentinian Luis Scola and Netherlander Dan Gadzuric. For most players in the game—all of them either in high school or of that age—the Summit was another chance to solidify their position in the pecking order for future drafts. Most players on the USA team would be headed off to the preeminent college programs in the country, while almost all of the members of the World team would head back to their respective countries, or various leagues around the globe, to play professionally.

Nowitzki, however, had a different plan in mind. Because, just two months after the Summit, the NBA Draft would take place in Vancouver, Canada. Nowitzki and his longtime mentor and coach Holger Geschwindner would be there, ready to bring his game to the NBA.

The Summit event, an annual showcasing of the game's brightest young stars, was his launching pad.

"Our dream was with the home team to go to the first division, get promoted, and we fell short every year. That year, again, we were in the promotion zone and we had big games," Nowitzki told ESPN in 2020 when recalling the buildup to the Summit.

Just making it to the games—let alone dominating them—would be an exercise in patience and creativity. "[We] had to ask permission from the [German] Army, because I was still in the Army, and I don't think you can travel out of the country unless you ask and it's for a big tournament or something. We had permission to go. Then we kind of had to ask the team. But Holger was kind of like, 'Ahhh, we'll just sneak out.' So I played the game Sunday night, and I think Monday morning we flew out of Frankfurt without really telling anyone. Holger might have talked to a manager or something, but I didn't say anything. So we snuck out."

He indeed snuck out, and, upon arriving in the United States—as he would do for many over the next nearly two decades—Dirk dazzled.

Against Team USA, whose roster was made up of some of the top high school players in the country, Nowitzki was easily the best player on the floor. Against future NBAers Erick Barkley, Al Harrington, Rashard Lewis, Quentin Richardson, and Stromile Swift, the 7-foot "German Wunderkind" was breathtaking, notching 33 points, 14 rebounds, 2 assists, and 3 blocks.

"That game really put me on the map. Back in the day, we didn't have Twitter or Instagram or all the social media stuff. Nobody knew who I was. I got invited to this game and it was a great experience for me," Nowitzki told the *Dallas Morning News* in 2019. "We got to go to the Final Four semifinals in the Alamodome which was an amazing, amazing experience. And I was able to play well in that game and all of a sudden had all this hype around me that I never had. Everybody said I was going to get drafted and I had like 40 college offers. It was an amazing time for me, a very exciting time. All of a sudden to be on the map in the U.S. That was amazing."

Geschwindner was confident that the Hoop Summit was the perfect opportunity for the NBA prospect to perform on the international high level, "because [Americans] had no idea how [good] he really was."

Donnie Nelson, who at the time was an assistant coach for the Dallas Mavericks, as well as the World team for the Summit, remembers vividly the impression Nowitzki made upon coaches when they first got an up-close glimpse of his skill set.

"He was one of the most gifted young players I'd ever seen, and besides all that, the guy was 7 feet tall. I mean, he was just an incredible basketball player! My concern was that he was too nice of a kid to be a killer. He's such a kind, big-hearted guy. Most of the guys that go into those forums are guys that would just as soon rip your heart out and show it to you. He didn't strike me as that kind of human being, so my concern was, 'Is he tough enough?' He certainly had the work ethic—you could tell."

The majestic hindsight of Nowitzki's career comes in waves. You can look back fondly on his killer instinct moments on the court (leading the Dallas Mavericks to the 2011 NBA Championship—the franchise's first—over the LeBron James-led Miami Heat) or his laid-back, relaxed personality. One such example was in a game against the Minnesota Timberwolves during the 2012 season when, while out of action to nurse an injury, Nowitzki joined the Mavericks' local television broadcast. When teammate Brandan Wright elevated to catch a lob pass from Jason Terry, Nowitzki—sensing the moment to come—raised his voice and, upon the completion of the dunk, yelled incessantly, "Shut it down, let's go home!"

It was the second quarter.

But his exuberant attitude was in-step with the boy who had arrived from Germany all of those year prior. His 7-foot frame silhouetted him as a larger-than-life figure; his perma-scowl on the court left opposing fans cursing his name; and his ability to perform in the clutch for the better part of his two decades in the league left an indelible legacy as perhaps the greatest international player of all-time.

To those closest, however, the gangly eighteen-year-old boy that arrived in 1998 never quite left. In fact, his first impression on teammates and staff members is one never forgotten among the Mavericks faithful, and one that wraps up in a bow the man known affectionately as "Dirk Diggler."

During the 1998 season, after the Mavericks' plane touched down in Seattle to open the lockout-shortened season—Nowitzki's first—the rookie received his itinerary from team personnel. Befuddled, he approached teammate Gary Trent with one simple question: *What is a shoot-around?*

"Shoot-around is like a rehearsal," a bemused Trent offered back.

Simple enough, right?

Not for Nowitzki. Before he had scored a point in the league, before winning the MVP a title, and all the memories, he still had one more question to offer up to the veteran Trent.

"What's a rehearsal?"

Over 20 years, 31,560 points, 14 All-Star appearances, an MVP award, and an NBA championship, Nowitzki proved to be the culmination of what so many promising international players before him promised to be but, for circumstances often outside their control, never fulfilled. He was the unfinished business of Arvydas Sabonis and Dražen Petrović.

Does he get lost in the annals of time, despite his nearly unprecedented resume?

Yes.

Does he belong squarely in the discussion as perhaps the most well-rounded player to ever play in the NBA?

Yes.

Do his accomplishments get downplayed due to his nationality, and that he wasn't American-born?

A fair argument can be made to that point. But as time goes on, and more foreign-born players make their presence felt in the upper echelon of the NBA, it's safe to assume that Nowitzki's legacy will shine brighter, too.

Chapter Four

EURO STYLE

"Some say you have to use your five best players, but I found out you win with the five that fit together best as a team."

—Red Auerbach

Auerbach's philosophy has been adopted and hammered throughout sweaty gyms across Europe, repeated by hoarse-voiced coaches as far as the ear can hear. But the simplicity of it has impacted the game of basketball across the Atlantic, invading the NBA over the past few decades, transforming a plodding, boring league built on slugfests and one-on-one sloggings into the fast breaking, no-look passing—and, most aesthetically pleasing—flair that the league is today. It's the flair for drama; flair for the sleight of hand; flair for making the impossible look, well . . . human.

It's that newfound spectacle that has led to events like Steph Curry's pregame showcase, when the twenty-first century's version of Pete Maravich unloads a flurry of one-off dribbles, two-ball handles, and 40-foot three-pointers. Fans are privy to watching a player who has more fun doing his job than almost anyone, and who has become must-see for wide-eyed kids straining to catch a glimpse of the awe-inspiring show. A show that has become more memorable, perhaps, than even the games themselves.

Curry is arguably the most transcendent star in the NBA today. He's the most impactful star the league has groomed since Jordan took flight in the mid-1980s. But Curry differs from "His Airness" in ways that have brought a new appreciation and electricity to the sport: because of his slight stature, Curry is more akin to the every-man than many of his contemporaries.

What separates Curry from the pack, and bonds himself with today's youth, is that he doesn't tower over his competition. He's not a 7-footer. He doesn't possess God-given natural athletic ability that leaves normal folk slack-jawed. Curry's gift to the game comes from watching, learning, digesting, and dissecting every aspect. He took pieces of his father Dell Curry's shooting stroke (it was easy since they shared a roof). He watched how Jason Williams performed magic tricks with the ball, often leaving his defenders tied up in string. He studied the precision in which players such as John Stockton and Jason Kidd placed their passes to where teammates needed them most.

Curry's game most resembles that of which you might find in a cramped gymnasium somewhere outside the United States. His style is straight-European; his game predicated on making his teammates better versions of themselves. And his influence is being felt now more than ever, as more and more young players are coming to the NBA from outside its normal footprint, ready to make the league their own.

Rick Barry, himself a Golden State Warriors legend, who has been involved with the NBA and international leagues for more than fifty years, tells me that the rise of the international superstar was inevitable.

"I saw what the potential of [European players] could be, and finally the NBA opened their eyes and started bringing more of those guys over here, and they've got a lot of outstanding players coming from all different countries."

Barry is unfiltered, and energetic beyond his seventy-six years of age. But when he takes a breath and looks at the NBA in 2020 from a 10,000-foot view, even he is almost at a loss for words when he sees how the league differs from the one he played in during his heyday.

"Some of the top players in the league today are all foreign. You just keep going down the list of guys who have come over and been incredible."

* * *

Perhaps most beneficial to Curry was the era in which he came into the NBA. When he first entered in the summer of 2009, it was at the tail end of a joyless and unwatchable era for the league. For example, that previous year the Utah Jazz led the league in assists per game, when they averaged just over 26 as a team (In in 2019, Curry's tenth season, his Golden State Warriors led the league with an average of 29.2.)[5] The numerical difference between the two doesn't appear to be drastic at first glance, but it's symbiotic of the style teams were playing. The Jazz were maestros of the pick-and-roll; efficient, but lacking creativity and ball movement. Since then, as coaches with international backgrounds or ideologies influence the league more and more—such as Mike

---

5   Furthermore, of the five highest APG averages by a team in league history, Curry's Warriors hold four of those records: first (2016–17: 30.4), second (2018–19: 29.4), third (2017–18: 29.3), and fifth (2015–16: 28.9) place.

D'Antoni and Steve Kerr—the NBA is passing more than ever, and players like Curry—sorceresses with the sphere, more adept and comfortable in open spaces—are thriving because of that influence.

"Curry's still-exploding pyro-cumulus cloud of popularity is such that people arrive early to Warriors games just to watch his *drills*," wrote Sally Jenkins for the *Washington Post*, "in which he alternates an entrancing parabolic shooting form with a conjuring athleticism so shape-shifting and yet sweetly balanced that even legendary Warriors executive Jerry West, the sublime shot-maker whose silhouette is on the NBA logo says, 'I'd pay to see him play.'"

And already, Curry's influence on the game of basketball is obvious. His unique style of play, for all intents and purposes, is becoming *the* game.

* * *

When they were drafted two picks apart—then swapped for each other in the 2018 NBA Draft—Luka Dončić and Trae Young had little idea their futures would be tied so intimately together. And just months after that trade went down, the immediate fallout was that it was an all-time hoodwink by the Dallas Mavericks and Luka Dončić.

While Dončić, a star in his home country of Slovenia who had played professionally since the age of sixteen, shot out of the gate to open his rookie campaign, Young, who had played one year at Oklahoma, struggled to find his footing.

Pocket-sized at just 6-foot-1 and 180 pounds, the former Sooners star had entered the league as a polarizing prospect. Some scouts looked at him as, if all went right, the next version of Steph Curry; some saw him as a knockoff version of Curry, one who would sink his team with his off-kilter and ill-aligned style.

Early on, as Young struggled with turnovers and a shot that refused to fall with consistency, Dončić flourished (which was to be expected; although of similar age, Dončić's five years of professional ball in Slovenia dwarfed Young's one season of collegiate ball at Oklahoma). Although just twenty years of age, his time playing professionally for Real Madrid had paid off in spades. Dončić slid effortlessly into the Dallas Mavericks starting lineup and, within weeks, had taken the NBA by storm. It was apparent early that the 6-foot-7 point-forward-do-all had, well ... it all.

Step-back threes? Check.

Court vision? Check.

Flair, drama, confidence? Check, check, and check.

Dončić would take home the Rookie of the Year Award, averaging 21.2 points, 6.0 assists, and 7.8 rebounds per game for the season.

Coming in second place, after his porous start, was Young. Dončić came straight out of central casting of what you envision in an international prospect: a full toolbox of skills. And with Young, fans were treated to the first true example of the effect that a player like Steph Curry had on the next generation.

And guys were ready to lead the NBA's next wave.

* * *

When you look at the scoring statistics for the EuroLeague for the 2015–16 regular season, one thing you'll notice is that the average of points per player is considerably lower than that of American games. For example, a great player in the NBA could average between 25 to 30 (or more) points per game on a season. For the EuroLeague, the highest average for the 2018–19 season by a player was 18 points. That player was Malcolm Delaney, who was born in the US.

Oh, and the leader for the 2018–19 NBA season was James Harden, who averaged 36.13 PPG.

One of the things the NBA has that the EuroLeague does not (which, in large part, contributes to the existence of most of the major differences) is the way the leagues schedule their games. When David Blatt, the former head coach of the Cleveland Cavaliers, was asked by *Business Insider* about the transition he had to make from coaching in Europe for 21 years to the NBA, he mentioned this exact point.

"Probably the schedule. Playing multiple games, the same week with very few practices, and having a different recovery process, is unknown territory. The good thing is ... trips are shorter and much smoother in the U.S." This change of pace is a struggle most European players face when making the same transition.

"By and large, these are the two primary differences between the leagues," Blatt said. "But where one may be lacking in one area, it makes up for in others. At the end of the day, it's all about enjoying and sharing the growing love for the sport."

But not everyone is convinced that the stylistic differences benefit the EuroLeagues more than the NBA. In 2006, Croatian-born Zoran Planinić was playing for the New Jersey Nets. During an interview, he told NorthJersey.com that teammate Nenad Krstić—who had played professionally in Serbia—was finding more success in the NBA than overseas because of the passing he found in America.

Although more and more international players were making a name for themselves in the NBA during the 2000s, they still struggled to gain the recognition that American-born players had. A Dirk Nowitzki or Manu Ginóbili would be outliers but, other than them, the marketing machine still focused on players born stateside. However, that began to change in earnest in 2014, when David Stern—after thirty years as the league's commissioner—stepped down, handing the reins over to Adam Silver, who had been under Stern as the league's deputy commissioner and chief operating officer for eight years. And with Silver at the helm, the NBA was set to embark on their most ambitious, forward-thinking wave yet. Silver was the opposite of what Stern had been. Where Stern had been cold and steadfast, Silver would be forward and outside the box.

Stern had been a controversial figure in his time running the NBA, but his contributions were undeniable. He could be at one time affable and energetic, and at others an extremist.

And, some would say ... well, let's go with "fickle."

As Ben Cohen wrote in the *Wall Street Journal*: "The league's longest-serving commissioner, Mr. Stern was as gruff as he was enormously influential when he was the most powerful man in basketball. He retired in 2014 and passed the NBA's stewardship to his longtime deputy, Adam Silver, after overseeing a period of growth that turned the NBA into the international behemoth it is today."

As he took over, Silver was complementary of the man he had studied under.

"Because of David, the NBA is a truly global brand, making him not only one of the greatest sports commissioners of all time but also one of the most influential business leaders of his generation," Silver said in 2019.

"The format we have now—I'm a traditionalist on one hand, but on the other, it's 50 years old or so, presenting an 82-game schedule, and there's nothing logical about it," says Silver. While the words that come from his mouth may have been eyebrow-raising, they came from a place of visionary-viewing.

* * *

He doesn't sport a curl-tipped mustache, slicked down with oil to twist on as he stares blankly out his 78th floor of his office. He doesn't cock his grin to the side, dethroning his enemies with an evil smile. He doesn't bludgeon anyone with outlandish fits, with spit and four-letter words flying in piston-like precision. And although he carries all the ferociousness of a shy accountant who looks as if he would cower were you to offer any feedback, Silver's words of moving away from the traditions that have both raised up, and leveled out, the NBA was directly in line with the way he sees the future of the league.

But when Adam Silver speaks his vision of the NBA into the open, the message that emits is one of a man envisioning complete totality.

Picture in your mind a great and powerful leader, a person tasked with guiding one of the biggest organizations in the world. Perhaps they have broad, powerful shoulders. A thick chest, which constantly puffs outward. A booming voice with just one engaged tone: dominance.

Now, when it comes to Silver, picture the opposite.

And yet, contrary to all of this, he may be the most forward-thinking visionary in all of sports. Because Silver isn't content with the status quo; simply raking in billions of dollars leaves him feeling flat.

Silver wants more. If the NBA under his watch isn't moving forward, it's not standing still; it's moving sideways, ready to career off the edge, alongside the AAF, XFL (v 1.0 and 2.0), and any other league that didn't make it. That won't happen to the NBA any time soon, but it's how Silver rolls. He's not content to sit back and let the NFL run a monopoly over the sporting world. He doesn't want European futbol to lay claim to the biggest game in the world and have any merit be behind it. Hell, knowing Silver, he has one eye on cricket, watching that from afar, eyeing their system of operations.

"I believe we can be the No. 1 sport in the world," he said in 2019.

"The NBA has done a great job of capitalizing on pioneers. Dirk. Hakeem. Guys from that 1980s or 1990s, who helped spark the new era," Ben Golliver of the *Washington Post* tells me. "Another aspect I don't think gets talked about enough is the rule changes. It's the soccerization of basketball. In hindsight, it's crazy how long it took these ideas to happen."

And it's happening now because of Silver.

* * *

Simon Chadwick, a sports enterprise professor at Salford Business School in Manchester, England, urged caution when relying too much on data coming out of China, which indicated that basketball was on track to be the most popular sport in the country. Chadwick said the NBA's benchmark in China is obvious, but that the league still needs to work hard "in new and emergent sports markets" if Silver's hope of basketball supplanting soccer is going to be realized.

"Getting the strategy right across these different territories is going to be a crucial factor in any potential growth in basketball's global popularity," Chadwick said. "Will basketball become the world's favorite sport? It is not inconceivable, although it is unlikely—at least in the short to medium-term. It will need nurturing, careful management, sound strategy, and good judgment if it is to succeed."

Taking on any sport or league outside of the NBA is not out of the question for Silver. In his mind, perhaps rightfully, the

NBA—and basketball in general—is the top dog. The sport of basketball also has the youngest average age by fan; the younger generations are finding more interest in basketball than other sports (baseball, for reference, has the oldest).

"When I look at the trajectory of growth, the fact that young people, boys and girls, continue to love this sport, are playing this sport, are engaged in the sport of basketball on social media or with online games, I don't know what the limit is."

"We know what the future looks like," NBA deputy commissioner Mark Tatum told NBC Boston in 2018. "When you look at China, India and Africa, you've got about 60 percent of the world's population in those three places. So, we're putting a lot of time and energy in how we become the No. 1 sport in those countries and those continents."

Silver's handling of the Covid-19 virus in the spring of 2020, when he was the first commissioner to cancel their events in the beginning of the outbreak, showcased his forefront-thinking, but also long-term game plan. The NBA has a relationship with China, and the tragedies that had befallen them were on the front of Silver's mind, along with the health and safety of his players, and the fan base, back at home.

"Right now, our focus is on working with global health organizations to provide whatever assistance we can to the people of China in response to the coronavirus outbreak," Silver told the *New York Times* in February 2020. "Many of our Chinese partners were unable to attend our N.B.A. All-Star events because of travel restrictions, but all of the weekend's events will be carried in China on Tencent."

This had come after the NBA and China found themselves at odds late in 2019, as protests spread throughout Hong Kong over police brutality, economic and social inequality, and a host of other issues. Like many other business in the United States, a large chunk of money coming into the NBA was directly via China, and the protests—as well as the Chinese government's handling of it—caused a rift in the front offices of the NBA, players who held marketing contracts in China, and a host of other folks.

The relationship had to be rebuilt. By 2020, the love affair from fans and the NBA had already grown to levels that were beyond reproach. And after the death of Kobe Bryant, long viewed as the perhaps most famous athlete in China (alongside Yao Ming), it was imperative that the NBA not lose the relationship and the 1.386 billion people that live there.

"I run into people here and they find out I work for the NBA and they say, 'I love Steph Curry or Ben Simmons and they tell me different things about the game," Derek Chang, then CEO of NBA China, told NBC Boston. "It's no different than being back in the U.S. and listening to sports radio in the morning. The intensity, the passion for it, it's pretty unbelievable. It really is a global game."

* * *

The Chinese Basketball Association (CBA) kicked off its inaugural season in 1994 and, since that moment, a series of events have led the league in becoming, arguably, the most sought-after location outside of the NBA. What the CBA lacked for in history and top-flight talent, they made up for in glamorizing themselves in other ways: their salaries were top-flight; they specialized in beginning-over stars (such as Stephon Marbury) to showcase the type of ball being played; they opened their doors to players during the 2011 NBA lockout; they plowed through while the struggling European economy threatened to dispatch players from the EuroLeague; and they cozied up to the NBA and its stars, making it the top destination for players looking for new marketing opportunities.

And for players just on the fringe of an NBA roster, on the outside looking in, China offered a new opportunity to brand themselves.

"They wanted to get NBA players, but there were no NBA players going to China," John Spencer, who played in China during the initial years, told *Bleacher Report* in 2013. "I was the closest thing in 1996 that had seen an NBA court."

As the league began in its infancy, they faced the same hiccups most start-ups do. Their resources were scant, and the conditions were rough—"I could tell you stories and you would pass out," Spencer says—but the magnanimous vibe of the league, and kind spirit of the Chinese people, were instant draws.

Spencer and his American comrades enjoyed a rare feeling, one that had remained a mistress in America: in China, they were celebrities. Everywhere they went, the fans treated them like heroes, referring to them often as Michael Jordan, Michael Jackson, or Mike Tyson.

"The thing about basketball in China has less to do with what happened on the court, but the passion of the fans in China," Spencer continued. "They appreciate what you bring to the table, and that's why the Americans like going there, because the Chinese fans are so appreciative of what you bring to the game—your passion, your skills, your desire, your hard work. That's what makes the country so special. It's an amazing place."

During the years that followed, as the CBA sustained its growth, the bonds between the NBA and China increased exponentially. Yao Ming's arrival in 2002 enhanced the relationship ten-fold, ushering in arguably the biggest romance between league and foreign entity.

If the NBA had been popular in China before—and if American players were idolized for their skillset and semi-fame—after Yao's arrival, the dam broke.

"What we have in Yao Ming is a global opportunity," Bill Sanders, director of marketing for BBA Sports Management of Los Angeles, who previously worked with the Houston Rockets, told the *Houston Chronicle* in 2002. "And so we feel strongly that the only real mistake we can make is to rush things. If we are patient, we'll be in great shape."

His vision was correct. The Rockets would be—and remain to this day—the most popular NBA franchise in China. And although the franchise and China are at odds after the controversy that arose over general managers Daryl Morey's comments of the protests in Hong Kong in 2019, the Rockets will forever be tied at the hip to the country, assuring that the franchise—and, by extension, the league—will profit long into the future.

In 2020, it was reported that some 300 million people in China—with a population of 1.4 billion—play basketball. The popularity of the game as a whole has seen widespread growth all over the world, but nowhere has that been more obvious than in China. And the NBA has been the biggest benefactor. In 2008, the league launched "NBA China," which overlooks the league's business in the country. It is now worth more than $4 billion, according to *Forbes*.

* * *

Adam Silver has long been known as an advocator and fan of the English Premier League; both the sport of soccer, as well as the operations of the league, from its fast pace, to the easily digestible nature for fans. Because of that, Silver has been forward thinking in how he wants the NBA to evolve, from proposing a midseason tournament for the NBA, to shorter and less frequent timeouts, or potentially even shorter games. The initial feedback (as you can imagine) from both fans and players alike was negative, but Silver's ideology is well-respected from owners and players alike.

"I recognize I'm up against some of the traditionalists who say no one will care about that other competition, that other trophy, you create," says Silver. "And my response to that is, 'Organizations have the ability to create new traditions.' It won't happen overnight."

The feedback primarily revolved around the fact that the NBA, for the most part (with certain exceptions dotting the globe), is filled with the best collection of talent, and that the ultimate end-of-year prize—the NBA championship—would render any additional tournaments, or "bonus titles," useless.

"In Europe, teams focus on the total rotation, team type of game. EuroLeague is an amazing competition, with a lot of great players as well," says Josh Powell, whose career has spanned all over the NBA, China, and Europe. "The competitive nature, the way the game is played is different. The atmospheres are also totally different. In the NBA, the teams don't deal with the same amount of pressure that the teams in Europe deal with, because every game is important, every game is played like it is a playoff game.

"But [the NBA] is the best. It's the best league in the world for a reason; the idea of basketball is a lot different," says Powell. "The best athletes, talent and everything else are at that level. It's similar to the CBA in the sense that it is a more individual league, and also shares some rules. As Luka Dončić said, it's easier to score in the NBA. The way guys compete is different, the three-second rule makes a huge difference, as the lane is much more open. The NBA is a much more relaxed environment when it comes to games because there are so many games."

* * *

The level of competition is rising in leagues all over the world. As the game expands and technology grows, shortening even more the divide of communication and opportunity, it's more and more apparent that—while the NBA will always be *the NBA*, and never likely be overtaken—opportunities are arising for players to make a lucrative and successful career elsewhere.

Case in point: after the NBA Finals took place in Canada in 2019—where the Toronto Raptors defeated the Golden State Warriors—Silver touched on the impact that could have in growing the game, which will do wonders for all leagues involved.

"I think symbolically," Silver said, "having our first Finals outside the United States maybe has a big impact on countries that follow the NBA but don't have teams, whether that be in Asia or whether that be in Latin America. So, I think as we look back in time at the NBA calendar, I mean, this clearly is a marker of sorts."

Leigh Steinberg, super-agent and source material for the movie *Jerry Maguire*, speaks to the rise in quality of foreign-born players as the league raised its international outreach.

"As basketball was popularized overseas in Europe and other places, it stared to produce a number of high-profile, foreign-born players, who's countries followed their journeys as they came to the NBA.

"It's not just that it attracted players who were good; it's bringing over dominant players. And for the NBA, those 108 players are just a walking advertisement for the league, going to those 42 different countries every night."

In fact, after the 2019 season, foreign-born players dominated the NBA awards. Giannis Antetokounmpo won the league's MVP; Luke Dončić was named Rookie of the Year; Rudy Gobert, of France, was named Defensive Player of the Year. Pascal Siakam won Most Improved Player. Antetokounmpo and Nikola Jokić were named First-Team All-NBA. Everywhere you turned, it was evident the NBA had morphed, seemingly overnight, into the World's game.

And, as Steinberg points out, it shows no signs of slowing down. Because while other sports take more coordinated efforts to play (baseball), or require vast amounts of equipment, players, and come with myriad safety risks (football, hockey), basketball stands out, alongside futbol, as perhaps the most simplistic sport to play, which carries massive appeal in parts of the world where resources are scarcer.

"Give David Stern, and later Adam Silver, for tremendous vison in understand that they had a sport that was easy to play," says Steinberg. "All you need to do to play basketball is have a ball. The barriers to access is much less. If you have a backboard and a basket, and you can afford a ball…you don't elaborate stuff."

And the impact it could have in the long run in places like China, specially, are not to be overshadowed.

"This is something Yao [Ming, the former Houston Rockets player who was born in China] and I have discussed, where we can use basketball maybe in the way ping-pong was used in the days of Richard Nixon," Silver told NBA.com writer Steve Aschburner in 2019, "that there could be something called 'basketball diplomacy.' And it is an area where our two countries have excellent history of cooperation, where we work closely with the Chinese Basketball Association on player development, referee development."

Before Covid-19 brought the world to a halt in March 2020, the World Cup of Basketball was to be staged in China in September 2020, and before that, the Chinese national team was to compete in the Las Vegas Summer League in July 2020. Those—and other initiatives—were designed to spur the game's continued growth there.

"Also, we are in the process of building academies in China to help develop the young players," Silver said. "Because of Yao's experience in the NBA, he sees how it's done, not just in the United States but in other places in the world. I think he understands that given the enormous number of young people, boys and girls, playing basketball, there's more that we can be doing to develop elite players."

When Yao Ming entered the NBA in 2002 as the first-overall pick by the Houston Rockets, the franchise envisioned the 7-foot-6 center as not just the heir apparent to Hakeem Olajuwon, but, potentially, a revolutionary player who would capture the imaginations of fans across the globe.

The key to the league's survival—and, miraculously, growth—after Jordan's retirement in 1998, came in the 7-foot-6 packaging of Yao Ming.

"Fortunately for the league, about the time Michael Jordan retired, Yao Ming came into the NBA," says Steinberg. "He was a figure of such enormous popularity in China that his presence alone set off a basketball frenzy in China and the Far East. The handsome, articulate, major star who played for the Shanghai Sharks. Coming from that enormous city, with that extraordinary population, that was a major factor in popularizing NBA basketball [in China]."

Yao's arrival in the NBA after his career in China (he played professionally from the age of seventeen when he joined the Shanghai Sharks of the Chinese Basketball Association) was a celebration for all involved. Although there were concerns about his ability to hold up over a full schedule (stop me if you've heard that one before; Yao had already broken his foot twice before coming to America), the Rockets we're getting him at a young age (he was just twenty-two years old)—and with a built-in financial boom: Yao, undeniably, was the biggest star in China, a country whose population at the time was 1.284 billion, even more so than Ichiro Suzuki and Hideki Matsui, and even Hideo Nomo before them, for Japanese players coming to Major League Baseball.

But while the experiment worked seamlessly for the first few seasons—the Rockets would make the playoffs in four out of his first seven years, and Yao would average 19 points and 9.2 rebounds during his career—his legacy is defined by what he showcased for short periods of time before succumbing to injuries (as has been the case for many big men). Foot deteriorations would force Yao to officially retire in 2011.

Chapter Five

THE DREAM TEAM EFFECT

Four years before the 1992 Summer Olympics, the Soviet Union, which took home a "questionable" gold medal at the 1988 Olympics (the final Olympics to take place without the involvement of professional basketball players from the United States), began loosening their restrictions on elite players from countries like Lithuania and the former Yugoslavia (which were both known as fertile grounds for young and upcoming basketball players).

The loosening of these restrictions allowed such stars as Dražen Petrović, Vlade Divac, and a handful of other Eastern European standouts to head west to the United States. There, they not only stood next to the giants of the NBA, but, in many cases, were just as talented, competitive, and skilled as their American-born counterparts.

By the start of the 1997–98 season—which would be the final season of Michael Jordan's Chicago Bulls career before he hung his sneakers up for a second time—30 international players who had come straight to the NBA were on opening-night rosters.

The original Dream Team took the 1992 Summer Games by storm with the likes of Jordan, Magic Johnson, Charles Barkley, Larry Bird, and a who's who of Hall of Famers around them (plus recently graduated Duke star Christian Laettner).[6] They were the biggest stars in the sport. In addition, because of the unique concoction of talent—for that summer, at least—they were arguably the biggest stars in the world.

By 2010, eighteen years after the games had concluded with a predictable American gold, 81 players from 41 different countries and territories were on NBA rosters during the course of the season. Kids who were born in the mid-to-late 1980s and were at their most impressionable in 1992 saw, for the first time, the sheer star power and celebrity that being a professional basketball player could bring you. "[The Dream Team were] the Beatles and the Rolling Stones all mixed into one," said Matt Zeysing, curator of the US Olympic Teams exhibit at the Naismith Memorial Basketball Hall of Fame.

"As a kid watching the NBA, I remember when Larry's Celtics would go overseas or Magic and the Lakers, and they would play Brazil, or Russia, or Lithuania, and those players were all very fundamentally sound, but they didn't have history," Sam Amico, a sportswriter for *Sports Illustrated*, tells me. "For them, basketball was still kind of new to being a competitive sport. But you got the sense that, when the Dream Team got together, that really opened up the rest of the World's eyes, and people said, 'Hey, this game is pretty cool.' But that's when people across the globe started falling in love with the superstars, and I think, for kids—because

---

6   Of the 12 players on the Dream Team, 11 are in the Naismith Memorial Basketball Hall of Fame, while Christian Laettner is in the College Basketball Hall of Fame.

if you look now, guys in their mid-thirties now, that's when they would have been impressionable. That was the first wave."

That summer was memorable for myriad reasons, many of which still resonate today. The global impact for basketball is first and foremost, but it was also a passing of the torch in many ways. While the Dream Team was filled with the game's best, it was the perfect blend of old and new. Though such stars as David Robinson, Barkley, Karl Malone, and John Stockton were in the middle of their prime, the team had two other halves: the future of the NBA in Jordan, Scottie Pippen, and Patrick Ewing, with the final shining moment for the old timers in Bird and Magic.

"This was our final moment—the curtain was going to come down. Larry's back was messed up and I was already out, dealing with HIV, so we had to make sure that we went out the right way," Magic Johnson told *GQ* in 2012. "For me, it was also about showing the world that I could still play, even living with HIV."

Perhaps the most enlightening moment to come from that summer—and it's a shining light on where things were at the time, and how far they've come—was the reaction from opposing players toward their American opponents.

"We felt like we were the luckiest guys in the world. We were going to play against the best, but also against African Americans— our little cousins from America," Herlander Coimbra, who played for the Angola national team in the '92 Olympics, told *GQ* in 2012. "During warm-ups we tried spectacular dunks to show them that we could play like in the NBA. They didn't dunk even once. They were really serious, all business."

The Dream Team won by an average of 43.75 points per game on their way to the medal stand. It was by far the largest divide between countries up to that point and would prove to be the pinnacle of American dominance. The fallout since, of course, has been a worldwide dedication to making sure America was never able to dominate like that again. With it, all involved parties have benefited—America, perhaps, the most.

Although the Dream Team was rarely challenged that summer, and the whole spectacle was more of a one-team showcase than anything else, there was one vendetta that two members of the team entered one game ready to act upon. And it was one that would pay dividends down the road, in turns out, right back in the city of Chicago.

* * *

"You ever watch a lion or a leopard or a cheetah pouncing on their prey?" asks Karl Malone. "We had to get Michael [Jordan] and Scottie [Pippen] out of the locker room, because they were damn near pulling straws to see who guarded him."

The "Him" in question was a young standout from Croatia named Toni Kukoč, whom the Bulls had drafted back in 1990 and was rumored to be finally heading to the Windy City.

Kukoč—who would win three titles with the Chicago Bulls (1996–98) and win the NBA's Sixth Man Award in 1996—was a decorated player long before he stepped foot in the NBA.

A three-time EuroLeague champion, four-time "Mister Europa Player of the Year," three-time "Croatian Sportsman of the Year," as well as being named to both the FIBA "50 Greatest Players" and "50 Greatest EuroLeague Contributors" lists, Kukoč's resume far outshone some of the more decorated NBA stalwarts.

Jordan, unsurprisingly, was unflinching in his desire to shut down Kukoč and send the message directly. "Hey, guys. Kukoč. Leave him for Scottie and me."

For Jordan and Pippen—who had already won back-to-back titles—He was a slap in the face from their general manager Jerry

Krause. He was an outsider to a cohesive unit; an extra cog for an already well-run machine. He was, perhaps most vital at that time, another paycheck to lighten other players' wallets.

Part of—or perhaps most of—Pippen's disdain toward Kukoč was filtered through Krause, who had continuously put off signing Pippen to an improved contract when he was, arguably, the second-best player in the NBA. Furthermore, members of the Bulls' front office—including Krause—traveled often to Croatia to convince Kukoč to join the team, even offering him more money than what Pippen was making at the time.

"Krause was recruiting this guy and talking about how great he was," Pippen told sportswriter Sam Smith in 2020. "You know that's like a father who has all his kids and now he sees another kid that he loves more than he loves his own. So, we were not playing against Toni Kukoč, we were playing against Jerry Krause in a Croatian uniform.

"I can't put Krause out on the court," Pippen continued. "I shook [Kukoč's] hand before and after the game. There's no bad blood between us." But the message that the two Bulls players wanted to send—*if you're going to join us, this is what it's like*—was delivered. Hard.

"I've never seen that kind of defense before," a bewildered Kukoč said after the game. He entered the matchup on July 27 anxious to face his future teammates; after his dreadful performance in which he shot just 2-for-11 from the floor while committing 7 turnovers (thanks to the ball hawking defense of Jordan and Pippen), he understood the message.

"They just wanted to prove to me how it is to play in the NBA. One game is not a test. I can play much better. After this game, I'm sure I have to improve my game. All parts."

Pippen says it was never personal, and the message was a direct delivery to Krause, not Kukoč. This was long before many international players had come over to the NBA and made immediate impacts.

"Americans didn't understand how tough people like Toni Kukoč were," commentator Michael Wilbon said in the Chicago Bulls' documentary *The Last Dance*, which ran on ESPN in the spring of 2020. "They had no idea. These people had no idea about the war-torn situations and the poverty and the oppression that guys like Kukoč came from. That produced them. That hardened them. And so it was stupid to call him soft. He had to fight to gain their respect—and he did it. "

Outside of Dražen Petrović, and, at the time, Vlade Divac, players like Kukoč were still much more of an unknown than a smart gamble. And for Pippen, Jordan, and the rest of the Bulls squad back in Chicago, there was still a hint of an America-first, everyone-else-be-damned attitude.

"I always thought about the NBA," Kukoč said to Sam Smith in 2020. "We were playing national teams and beating USA national teams, beating Russian teams. We all got drafted [by NBA teams]. First Drazen went and Vlade; others went, but they did not play, [Sasha] Volkov, [Zarko] Paspalj. The problem was opportunity. Guys were afraid. Would I go to a Chicago Bulls team winning a championship and I might be sitting on the bench and not playing for the best part of my career? Maybe at 31 or 32 it would be worth it; not at 24. Jerry Krause, he said, 'No, no, no, you will see, you'll get a rebound and have Michael run one side and Scottie will run the other side. You will use your talents. Your game is suited to us.'"

"I had to change my game completely," Kukoč continued. "I was what Scottie was. What he was doing here, I was doing in Europe. When Michael retired, I had a chance to be a secondary guy; I had some freedom [averaging his most points until after Jordan's second retirement]. I had never played the power forward position. I knew certain people would massacre me with their power. They could physically destroy me. So, on the other end, I could do it to them.

"Michael, Scottie, and Dennis didn't change. Instead of someone saying, 'OK, I trust you,' it was Tex [Winter, an assistant coach] telling me, 'Don't shoot, don't dribble.' Then I hit a couple of shots and he says we need more of that."

Since then—after three NBA championships among the trio from 1996 to 1998—the views have changed. Now, Pippen—the man who single-handedly set out to embarrass Kukoč on the biggest stage imaginable—is the leader in championing his former teammate for a spot in the Basketball Hall of Fame.

"I definitely think he deserves it," Pippen said to Smith. "He was a huge piece for us. You look at the game today, teams have the Big Three now. Toni was a part of that puzzle for us. He was productive and deserves a lot of credit for our success."

It was also the first sign of the tide turning toward American dominance that summer.

* * *

The initial point of the Dream Team—allowing pros to participate in the Olympics after decades of amateurism—was controversial at first glance, with many wondering if America was trying to buy their way to a gold medal, especially after the 1988 team fell short, which was the final time they would use amateurs while the rest of the world sent professionals. It was clear that in order to keep up with what the rest of the World was doing, the days of America sending over amateur players (mostly from college) were over.

The controversy, as it were, was placed on the head of one Boris Stanković.

* * *

Odds are if you asked 1,000 die-hard basketball fans who Boris Stanković is, you might receive wildly inaccurate guesses. But Stanković, a former Yugoslavian veterinarian and meat-and-cheese inspector, is arguably the man most responsible for the global rise of basketball. In the late 1980s, tired of his fledgling career as a veterinarian, he ventured off to the United States on an "intelligence gathering" mission on the wings of FIBA, basketball's international governing body. Stanković had been bothered by the fact that the USA was not allowed to send over their best players (those from the NBA) while the rest of the world trained year-round, showcasing every four years the best they had to offer.

The biggest draw came from the fact that other countries were finding loopholes in sending their pros; most often, players listed "soldier" or "policeman" or "postal worker" as their profession, which allowed the teams to maintain their claims as "amateurs."

As Lorenzo Arguello wrote for *Business Insider* in 2012:

> Stanković returned to Europe and told his FIBA boss the organization's amateurs-only clause needed to be dropped so American superstars could participate in the Olympics and the game could grow on a global scale. Stankovic's suggestions were ignored, mostly because the assumption was that the International Olympic Committee [IOC] wouldn't budge. And it didn't.

"My concern was trying to make the game of basketball strong, to grow it, and yet there was this separation. It became impossible for me to tolerate," Stanković said to Arguello in 2012.

But persistence begets results, and the iconic Dream Team would shift the landscape of basketball around the world, causing a ripple effect that is felt more today than at any time before.

"It's certainly a global game now," Rick Barry tells me. "Soccer was the one that was there, and basketball is quickly encroaching on that, I think; it's always been the plan of the NBA to evolve. And when they finally allowed the pros to play in the Olympics, I believe, that was the turning point. And that was all because of Boris Stanković."

And at no time had it been more apparent than on a hot night in June 2019, with Giannis Antetokounmpo, a passionate and generational player, accepting his MVP Award, a world away from his humble beginnings in Greece. And the roots of his MVP season, indirectly linked back to the visions of Stanković, the impact of the Dream Team, and the ideologies of the league, are not lost on the "Greek Freak."

He knows first-hand the impact the summer spectacular can have; how much it means to countries around the world that are still searching for respect. Still trying to lay claim as the best in the world.

"I always feel something special when playing for the national team. When you are starting the tournament and listening to the national anthem, the emotions can't be described. After the first basket, the first plays, it is an amazing experience and every time I feel as proud as the first time," Giannis told the Greek newspaper *Ta NEA*, per EuroHoops.net. "The feeling of winning with the national team is incredible, and I have said before that I will always be part of the team, as long as I am healthy like this summer.

"I would exchange the MVP title for the gold medal in China [at the next Olympics]."

* * *

By opening night of the 2019 season, 108 players from 42 different countries—more than 20 percent of those in the world—were on NBA rosters. What was different in 2019 as opposed to 2010, or 1998, or any time before, was not just the volume of players, but their impact. No longer are American-born players controlling the impressionable youth; today, it's Giannis, a young man from Greece, a shy kid with Go Go Gadget arms and a work ethic that belies his athletic abilities. It's a big-grinned prodigy from Slovenia named Luka who is pushing for MVP honors at the age of twenty-one, while doing so in a way that reminds you that the game can be fun, too.

It's a 7-foot-3 big man from Cameroon named Joel Embiid, who overcame early signs of his body breaking down (and a debilitating Skittles addiction) to find himself atop the mountain for centers in the league.

It's a man named Nikola Jokić from Serbia, who comedian Ian Karmel once said is "what butter looks like if it were human," eradicating social norms about what body types are allowed to succeed in athletic competition.[7]

These young stars aren't just carrying the mantle until the next wave of youngsters come in to take it from them. Instead, they're usurping the title of the best in the world . . . and doing so in a manner not yet seen on American soil.

---

7   As of June 2020, Jokić had 40 triple-doubles in his career, which is 10th-most in NBA history, and more than any other foreign-born player. He's also twenty-five years old, and in his fifth full season.

Chapter Six

AWAKENING FROM THE DREAM

There are no quantitative facts to pull from when dissecting the impact the 1992 Dream Team had on the future of basketball. Sure, you could scour the internet for recreational league participation, or for participation numbers around youth basketball, but, unless every kid was polled prior to their first game and asked why they were there, you can still glean very little from those types of numbers. With that being said, it's almost impossible to deny the influence those 12 men had on an impressionable age group of boys and girls thirsting for heroes.

In America, yes, but primarily overseas.

"I think basketball was about to explode and the dynamite stick to explode was the Dream Team," US coach Mike Krzyzewski, an assistant on that team, said in 2015 to the Associated Press.

Coach K, as he is affectionately known, has been the head coach at Duke University since 1980, and perhaps has as big a pulse on how kids were influenced by what they saw that summer of 1992 as anyone. The way he runs the Duke program—which has won 15 ACC Championships, been to 12 Final Fours, and won five NCAA tournament national championships under his watch—is the closest thing America has to an NBA-ready program. The next best thing besides Duke might just be playing professionally overseas, which many of Krzyzewski's players have done.

"Duke is like an extension of the pros," Ricky Price, who played for the Blue Devils from 1994 to 1998, told GoDuke.com in 2012. "When you're playing at Duke, you're playing at such a high level. It's preparing you for the next level. For me, my overall dream was to play in the NBA. That never happened for me, but I was ultra-prepared to go overseas and play."

Krzyzewski's involvement in the 1992 Olympics, then, fit perfectly into the vision of the game, which was set to see its biggest global rebranding yet. And what it did for players around the globe was just as big; what it spawned was a new generation of players from countries all over the globe.

"It's because of guys like Dirk Nowitzki," Giannis recently told *Sports Illustrated* about who the new generation of talent looked up to when they were growing. "Pau Gasol, Tony Parker, Manu Ginobili, and those guys. Even older, Drazen Petrovic. They set the path for us."

What the 1992 Dream Team did for basketball—for the youth movement; for the rekindled passion in America; for the growing interest in other countries, who viewed those 12 Americans as something almost God-like—captivated the sports world long after all interested parties had returned home from Barcelona. Once the hangovers had left, and the tans had faded, there was still a league to tend to.

The 1992 Olympics "just all kind of changed everything," said Jerry Colangelo, chairman of USA Basketball. "It opened the door for a lot of people and then people started to jump into it."

What that summer also did—thanks to the vast amount of eyeballs that tuned in—was introduce a new generation of fans to the beautiful game that was being played all over the world. The United States may have run through the Olympics without breaking a sweat, but the way their opponents were playing the game was not lost on those who paid attention. And all these years later, the benefits have come in ten-fold.

"Now we've gone more that way, because there aren't that many good big post players to start out with," Rod Thorn, NBA president of operations, told AP in 2015. "We didn't have what is called a stretch 4 until we started getting all these kids from Europe. The Nowitzkis of the world in particular, guys who could shoot the ball out on the court and were big, and now everybody looks for a stretch 4."

And with the help of the breakaway star of that Dream Team—Michael Jordan—that's exactly what happened.

The 1992–93 NBA season would play out much like the previous two—with the Chicago Bulls, led by Jordan, Scottie Pippen, and Phil Jackson—raising the trophy. The first three-peat in the NBA since the Boston Celtics won eight titles in a row, from 1959 to 1966, was complete. Jordan was officially the biggest star in the sports world. Actually, it's pretty easy to say that he was not just the biggest in sports: he was arguably the biggest star in the world. Period.

When the Bulls notched their third straight title the season following the Olympics, there was already a seismic shift in how the game was being viewed.

"The finals in '93 between Phoenix and the Bulls, I think we probably had like 20 [Japanese] media, but '92 there were only me and the cameraman between the Bulls and Blazers," said AP journalist Yoko Miyaji.

* * *

Perhaps the best way to correlate the impact of the Dream Team comes from Jack McCallum himself, the man who literally wrote the book on them (*Dream Team: How Michael, Magic, Larry, Charles, and the Greatest Team of All Time Conquered the World and Changed the Game of Basketball Forever*). When asked about his views on why the Dream Team still carries so much weight, even all of these years later, McCallum told the Associated Press:

> That generation, it loomed above all others. Even if you didn't know who those players from 1992 were, and you were a fan of LeBron James and Kevin Durant, you endlessly heard LeBron and Durant referred to as Michael Jordan and Magic Johnson, and any white player who comes around, maybe Kevin Love, is referred to as Larry Bird. So, the frame of reference for basketball always seems to be these guys. These guys were accepted as basketball royalty, and therefore you didn't have to over-explain it. That's very helpful for a writer when he can be writing for someone who is 70 years old and hopefully be writing for someone who's 20.

* * *

What's in a shoe? More specifically, what's in a shoe's value, not monetarily, but intrinsically? What significance does it carry for generations of youth who stand slack-jawed outside department store windows, dreaming one day of dawning the latest trend wear on their feet?

When Jordan signed with Nike out of college in 1984, the shoe giant, which would move on to global domination in the years that followed, was not yet the Nike we all know today. Companies like Adidas and Converse (Jordan's shoe of choice during his playing days at North Carolina) were still considered the big hitters; Nike at the time was still in its infancy, having yet to fully jump into the sneakers game. And, much like the company he would sign with to kick start his NBA career, there was not yet proof that the young Jordan was set to take the (figurative) game to another stratosphere, ending his career, indisputably, as the greatest player to ever live.

So, in 1984, the battle for obtaining the rights to Jordan was a close one. Ultimately, Adidas' blunders were too much for Jordan to overlook.

"We're sitting in the conference room [with Adidas] and they're saying things like, 'We *are* basketball,'" Jordan's agent David Falk recalled later to ESPN's Darren Rovell. "They're telling us that they have Magic, Bird, Dr. J and Mark Aguirre."

The company's braggadocious foray into the world of Michael Jordan was tone deaf and out of touch. Jordan, even at the young age of twenty-one, sensed where his future could be, and wanted no part of sharing the light with the current faces of the NBA, which is what he would have been dealing with had he aligned himself with Adidas.[8] And although he wanted to be a part of Adidas, his visions were now bigger than being just another guy alongside Bird, Magic, and the rest of the company's stars.

---

8   Adidas and Converse had recently split after years of partnering.

"I give him a lot of credit," Joe Dean, who was in charge of Converse's marketing at the time, told ESPN in 2013. "He was asking, 'With all these stars, where do I fit into the conversation?'"

But the death knell for Adidas came when Jordan's father spoke up during a sit-down meeting and asked one simple question to the powers that be: "Don't you guys have any new, innovative ideas?"

Up to that point, the pitch to the Jordan clan had been too ... impersonal. If the company really wanted him—like, *really, really wanted him*—the recycled and clichéd pitches that had worked on older players like Bird and Magic had to go by the wayside.

The room fell silent.

It's all the Jordan family needed to hear.

Just like that, Adidas and Converse were out; Nike, forward thinking, hip, and willing to bend over backwards to please their prospective client, was in. In one decision, the landscape of sports and consumerism would be forever changed.

A few weeks later, Falk came up with the "Air Jordan" moniker, ostensibly igniting the most successful ad campaign in the pantheon of sports and putting Jordan and Nike in the most rarefied of, well ... air.

"Would the brand have been as strong if it was Adidas?" Jordan asked. "We'll never know."

Luckily for Jordan, Adidas' missteps had made that a moot point.

"In hindsight, it was perfect for me because it made my decision that much easier, and I ended up with Nike."

Leigh Steinberg speaks to the global effect of Jordan's partnership with Nike.

"You have to look at the shoe companies, and the fact that companies like Nike do an extraordinary amount of business all throughout the world, and what they sell primarily was, in the shoe market, basketball shoes," Steinberg tells me. "I've talked to Phil Knight about this—you can see the shoe on the basketball court, right? Sneakers, and the sneaker market, is huge. Companies would put heavy marketing dollars in overseas markets, which were built around, not just Jordan, but the next generations, all the way to LeBron James. It created huge stars in players like Kobe Bryant. These were ads with great production value; state-of-the-art ads which ran over and over. It not only popularized American players, but the concept of basketball."

Fast forward eight years. Standing on the podium among 11 teammates, Jordan, flanked by Bird and Magic, is cloaked in his team-issued Reebok warmup gear. Every available camera imagined is on him; over the course of the previous two seasons—especially the past few weeks—Jordan had rocketed past all competitors. He was, hands down, the star of the games, of the sport, and of the world.

As members of the Olympic committee went down the line, draping gold medals around the necks of each player, smiles glazed over their faces, Jordan had an idea, one he had crafted in his mind long before the confetti reigned down in celebration of their gold medal.

By the time they reached him, draped across his chest, covering the rival-Reebok logo, was an American flag. In arguably the biggest moment of his career, Jordan never lost sight of what mattered to him. The brand.

The brand would catapult him over for the next six seasons, which would see him lose his father, retire from basketball, take on professional baseball, only to return to the NBA and perform yet another three-peat with the Bulls.

* * *

It was up to the NBA, and the world at large, to capitalize on the unfathomable momentum the Dream Team had brought to the sport. When the league resumed play just two months later, they had a choice to make: continue to beat down the narrative that the NBA was vastly superior, that America was on another playing field, and use the cringeworthy performances of other countries during the Olympics as shining examples of that.

Or, they could go an alternative route and embrace the spotlight that the sport was thrust into. Although many of the games in Barcelona had been over by halftime, the players on the Dream Team could see firsthand that, sprinkled throughout the tournament, were talented, NBA-ready players. Players that, up until that point, had never experienced what a full-tilt NBA roster could look like.

As John Walters of *Newsweek* wrote in 2014:

> When the 1992 "Dream Team" defeated Croatia in the Olympic gold-medal game, the silver-medal Croatian team only had two players who had played in the NBA [Drazen Petrovic and Stojko Vrankovic], and three who would later join the league [Toni Kukoc, Zan Tabak, and Dino Rada.] Twenty years later, in the 2012 Olympics, the silver-medal Spain team had eight players who had played in the NBA [Pau Gasol, Rudy Fernandez, Sergio Rodriguez, Juan Carlos Navarro, Jose Calderon, Sergio Llull, Marc Gasol, and Serge Ibaka], and one who would later join the league [Victor Claver].

* * *

"Shit, I have no idea."

It's a loaded question with a simple answer for Jack McCallum, the legendary *Sports Illustrated* writer who is almost as synonymous with the Dream Team as the players

themselves. Jack is minutes away from scooting out the door
with his wife to babysit their grandchild. But, for now, he's
lost in his memory, flipping through the Rolodex. It has been
twenty-eight years since the most famous and infamous collection of talent took grip of the world in Barcelona during the
summer of 1992.

So, I ask again: *Could you have seen this coming eighteen years
ago, the depth and talent of international players coming to America,
and being the faces of the game?*

This time, the answer is no. And Jack, who was as close as
anyone to the Dream Team that summer, is not alone.

"Europe at the time was an incredibly fertile ground. They
had the NBA, but they really had it in bite-size nuggets," said
McCallum in a 2012 *Sports Illustrated* article. "They really had
only the appetizer, and what they were waiting for was the main
course. So, there was sort of a mystical, easy thing about the NBA
. . . and now they were going to see it in real life.

"And finally, these players, in terms of a sporting culture, were
as big as you could get. I think probably you could put LeBron
in that category now. Maybe Kobe and Shaq when they were
together. But you're talking about a time in our sport when guys
like Magic, Michael, and Larry were as famous as any athletes,
and the NBA was at the top of the sporting culture."

Whether they knew it or not, players around the league were
about to be inundated with fresh international talent, many of
whom had already been drafted and were biding their time to
come to America. After the Olympics, the time to pounce had
arrived.

Bob Whitsitt, who was the general manager for the Seattle
SuperSonics, told McCallum in 1991 that "it's a new development that's significant, and though we don't know what the long-
term ramifications are, we'd better be ready."

That season Whitsitt—who would go on to be the general manager of the Portland Trail Blazers when Arvydas Sabonis finally made his NBA debut—hired his first-ever European scout.

The first player to jump, with the biggest splash, was Kukoč. As McCallum wrote for *Sports Illustrated* ahead of the 1992 Olympics, "While the Bulls continue their multimillion-dollar courtship of Yugoslav star Toni Kukoč, the argument over whether foreign players will ever make a real impact in the NBA rages on. Most teams now have at least some semblance of a European scouting operation, yet the foreign players currently making major contributions in the league number exactly one— Vlade Divac, the Lakers' starting center."

As Kukoč recalled, the confidence of he and his teammates was never in question, even as the rest of the world may not have yet been on board.

> We were sure we could play in the NBA. But even when we came here people were like, they all are soft and don't play defense and they don't rebound. We started beating Americans all the time. Italy with the junior nationals beating them soundly, Seattle. We figured, "OK, these are the guys we are beating every time we play them. These are the guys who are going to be the top draft picks, the future All-Stars, the guys who are going to carry the league and we are beating them. So, it is time for us." But even when we came here people were like, "They all are soft and don't play defense and they don't rebound." Nobody said we had some many different skills other people don't. I wish I would have come here with a coach who said, "Here is the ball, we trust your decisions." Like you see now with Luka [Doncic], with [Nikola] Jokic, Giannis [Antetokounmpo]. They weren't ready for us then.

But if the hurdle for European players had been high before, it had been raised even higher by the Olympics setback. The reputation in NBA locker rooms for international players was—to say the least—less than stellar.

"Back then it was very difficult for we Europeans to prove to everyone we could play," admitted Divac to Sam Smith in 2020. "Now almost half the league are internationals. We had to fight for our time, for the way we played. But if you look at how basketball has evolved, it's more the game that suits us now, passing, transition, shooting. Which is why Toni is one of the most important people who changed the game."

The almost immediate successes of guys like Kukoč and Divac went a long way in changing the perceptions. Kukoč slid in seamlessly with the Bulls and was a pillar during their second run of championships, from 1996 through 1998. Divac never won a title with the Lakers, but he, too, fit right in alongside the "Showtime" Lakers.

"I'm glad we proved we knew the game," Kukoč continued. "We could not beat them physically, not beat them athletically. But we beat them fundamentally and with the skills. We are not going to try to dribble around them, we are not going to try to go over them. But we make a lot of screens, pass, and don't dribble a lot and try to find the right people at the right time."

And along the way, they even began to shape the way the game was being played instead of simply adjusting their style to fit the slower paced American style. As Kukoč explained:

I don't want to say which guard it was with the Bulls, but I would take the ball and he would come to me and say, "You are taking my bread." I didn't know the slang. I asked what he meant. I said I will give you the ball if you run down court and you can shoot and score. He said to me

I didn't understand. He was a point guard and I was taking his bread. He needed to average a certain number of
assists. So, it was hard for me at first. If I get a rebound
and have an open floor, why would I have to look for you
and have you come back to get the ball? Just run and you
will have a wide-open shot. But they didn't think that way.
There were a lot of adjustments.

Another pioneer in the European scouting game, Don Nelson,
who was the coach of the Golden State Warriors at the time, said
to McCallum in 1991, "It's different for them than for guys coming out of college, who spent their whole lives thinking about
playing in the NBA This is new ground for players from other
countries. They need time." But his observations were proving
to be more antiquated than based in reality. What players had
to do wasn't change their style, per se, but—as was the case with
Kukoč—adapt to the personalities they were teaming up with.

* * *

The Dream Team, it's safe to say, will not be forgotten. Nor
should they. Every player involved has etched their name in stone
among the greatest to ever play the game. Hell, even Christian
Laettner is revered for what he did as a college player. But for all
of their individual and team glories in the NBA and what they
pulled off that summer in Barcelona, their greatest impact may
just be the doors they opened up for young kids across the globe.

"Then the questions from the media and from teammates,"
said Kukoč. "'Can this guy actually play? Is he worth playing for
the mighty Bulls? This skinny communist Yugoslavian guy thinks
he's OK.' But when I think about it now and how everything has
developed and other players have come in, more power to them

with the recognition for guys like [Dirk] Nowitzki and [Tony] Parker and [Manu] Ginobili; we know what we did. They didn't think much of us back then, but we are the ones breaking the ice. It's always hard to be first. Someone has to do it, and we know we made it easier for the guys who came after us. And now you see how basketball is a global game and the NBA looks at someone and says, 'OK, he's a basketball player.'

"I would watch San Antonio play and see plays I recognized from the Russian team, the Yugoslavian team," Kukoč continued. "That's why I think [Gregg] Popovich was ahead of his time. He was never resistant to those plays and players. Now a coach can relay a message to the team. But back then could they say to Michael to give the ball to Toni? Can you imagine New York saying to [Patrick] Ewing and [John] Starks, 'OK, give the ball to that European guy?' Popovich, he went to Seoul, to Europe. He saw."

The world was now seeing, too.

Chapter Seven

BYE, BYE, JORDAN

In 1974, Al Green recorded the hit song "Take Me to the River"; a few years later, the soul singer diverted from his previous path, becoming an ordained minister at the Full Gospel Tabernacle Church in Memphis, Tennessee. He would henceforth be known as the "Reverend Al Green," finding popularity through various forms of music for decades more.

On January 1, 1999, Gemmy Industries released "Big Mouth Billy Bass," ostensibly igniting the biggest and most absurd pop culture craze of the year. The fish, dancing and flailing away in homes around the world, would belt out "Take Me to the River," lining the Rev's pockets deeper every day.

Twenty days later, following a 204-day lockout filled with rock-'em, sock-'em style infighting, multimillionaire spats, slaps, chokes, and a professional league barreling toward a PR nightmare, the NBA's strike came to an end. A 50-game schedule would begin 12 days later.

The post-Michael Jordan era, one the league had been silently preparing for since his ill-fated and short-lived first retirement in 1993, was underway.

And it was an all-out disaster.

When Jordan announced his retirement from the NBA on January 13, 1999, the Chicago Bulls were already in the process of tearing the dynasty down to nothing. Phil Jackson, the orchestrator of all six Bulls titles, was out, replaced by the irreparably in over his head Tim Floyd. Scottie Pippen and Dennis Rodman were expendable, if for no other reason than the franchise saw no point in paying for their services; without Jordan, winning was no longer the objective. Management had stripped the three-time defending champs down to a rebuilding project.

"Without Michael Jordan, the NBA has a serious problem," Leigh Steinberg told the Associated Press at the time. "It's difficult to imagine one player having more of an impact over a league. Some polls show him as the most widely recognizable person in the world. He has so much dominance that's not like someone is a close second."

With the cash cow Bulls fading quickly into oblivion, David Stern and the NBA faced more questions in a two-week span than they had faced in the entire Magic-Bird-Jordan twenty-year run. Other franchises, which had toiled away in the shadows of the Windy City, were tasked with helping both carry the league, while doing so out of the rubble they had created with the lockout, because the NBA wasn't just losing their iconic face; they were losing their most marketable franchise as well.

"I think without Michael Jordan it was going to be really, really hard for the NBA to get back to where it was," former NBA player Eddie Jones told EuroHoops.net in 2018.

In 1998, the two biggest brands outside of the Chicago Bulls—as was always the case—were the Los Angeles Lakers and Boston Celtics. That had been true for decades. When the two franchises were good (which they oftentimes were), it was a built-in moneymaker for the league. The East Coast-West Coast rivalry? Check. The two winningest franchises in league history? Check. All-time legendary players playing for both squads? Check.

But now? Crickets.

In the first season without Jordan, the Spurs-Knicks series drew the NBA Finals' lowest ratings in 18 years, down 40 percent from the Bulls-Jazz series the previous year, according to the *Los Angeles Times*.

The Lakers, giving credit where it's due, were doing their part. They sported two of the games brightest young stars in Kobe Bryant and Shaquille O'Neal, winning 61 games while finishing second in the Western Conference behind the Utah Jazz and tied with the Seattle SuperSonics. The core of their eventual dynasty enveloped those two players, as guys like Rick Fox, Robert Horry, and Derek Fisher formed a talented, veteran-laden roster. The Lakers were on the come-up.

Across the country, however, things were spiraling south. The Celtics had finished at 36–46, their fifth losing season in a row. Their glitzy hire of former University of Kentucky head coach Rick Pitino was already proving to be a bomb. The Celtics, perhaps the proudest franchise in the NBA, was in shambles. Their trio of stars from the 1980s—Bird, Kevin McHale, and Robert Parish—were long gone. New waves of talent such as Antoine Walker, Dee Brown, and Eric Montross were more sizzle than steak. They even tried bringing in Dominique Wilkins to revitalize a fledgling fan base. None of it was working.

So, heading into the 1998–99 season, with Jordan (and the Bulls) seemingly out, and the Celtics clearly out, the NBA faced a new realism. They would be, essentially, starting from scratch.

"From the perspective of business, I predicted if Michal Jordan came back it would mean tens of millions of dollars to the NBA, even in an abbreviated season," Dean Bonham, a sports consultant, said as word of Jordan's retirement was becoming known. "In the short term, this costs the NBA not only that money, but the ability to heal the wounds the lockout formed with their fans. The easiest and quickest way would be for Jordan to play in a swan song season. Long term, you're talking about an individual that *Forbes* [at the time] estimated had a $10-billion impact on this economy since he became a professional. The economic impact on the NBA over [the next] few years is probably immeasurable, but certainly in the tens of millions—if not hundreds of millions—of dollars."

Not everyone was as downtrodden on the long-term prospects as Bonham. "This league is going to succeed without Michael Jordan," Jerry West, the longtime Los Angeles Lakers general manager, told the AP in 1998. "Obviously, having him here would be good because of the negative things, and he seems to find a way to make all of those negative things go away. But to say the league is going to sink with Michael Jordan, it's just not the case."

"There is no question in my mind the NBA will continue to thrive and flourish irrespective of whether or not Michael Jordan is playing," Bonham continued. "The questions are to what level?"

The other issue—one that had been brewing, steadily, for a couple of seasons—was the eventual lockout the league was facing. If the owners and players association failed to come to terms on the myriad subjects they were up against, the first season sans Jordan would be delayed. An already deflated fan base would potentially be without basketball altogether unless the two sides came to an agreement.

When 12:01 a.m. struck on July 1, 1998, that was the reality. The two sides were still miles apart, and the league was officially shut down. The main battle, of course, was money. Although there had been two previous "stoppages" in the NBA over the previous three years, neither had resulted in games lost. The NBA, in fact, was the only league at that time to never had missed a game because of a labor dispute. But that was soon to change.

By the time the regular season was set to begin, the two sides were no closer to a deal than they had been over the previous year. The players, seeking a massive pay increase due in large part to the TV ratings explosion over the previous decade, wouldn't budge. The owners, looking to protect their collective bargaining agreement salary cap, wouldn't budge. It wasn't until January 6, 1999, just one day shy of then commissioner David Stern's final deadline before he claimed he would shut down the entire season, that the two sides came to an agreement. After nearly seven months of players being barred from practice facilities, training facilities, or anything to do with their respective organizations, the league was back.

* * *

One of the issues the league had to navigate coming out of the lockout was that, due to the shortened timeframe, teams would be playing 50 games in 90 some-odd nights. Not only that, but due to the fact that players had been kept out of the practice and training facilities, they were woefully out of shape. However, faced with no other options, back-to-back-to-backs would become the norm. It quickly took a toll on the players. "It's always been remarkable to me that we were still able to put a team out there every night," Lenny Currier, who was the Philadelphia 76ers' trainer in the early 2000s, told *The Ringer*. If fans in the stands felt the product was rushed, and that a subpar performance was being trotted out, it was backed up, almost nightly, with the action on the court.

With the league still navigating the waters between the tried-and-true method of pounding the ball down low, watching-the-big-man-back-in style and the new-age run-and-gun, games were, at times, unwatchable. Scoring was down four points per game from the previous season. With the barrage of games, the lack of rest, and the extensive travel, every game seemed to slog along in a tedious, boring manner.

"You know how guys say that the season is a marathon?" veteran guard Terry Porter told Thomas Golianopoulos of *The Ringer* in 2019. "Well, that year it was a sprint. It was a full-out sprint."

As Golianopoulos wrote, "The 1999 NBA campaign was unlike any other: free-agent signings and a 12-day training camp beginning simultaneously on January 21, leading up to opening night on February 5. The regular season consisted of 50 games in 90 nights, a grueling slog in an era before DNP-REST. Back-to-backs were the norm. Three games in three nights were common."

If losing Jordan and the lockout weren't enough, the NBA's PR department was working overtime on another issue. Although it has been over a year since the incident took place, the league was still being rocked by the Latrell Sprewell saga.

* * *

On December 1, 1997, just a few months after he arrived in Golden State, Sprewell—despondent over what he perceived as a lack of playing time, a lack of a clear and defined role, and, seemingly, the entire operation as a whole—choked head coach P. J. Carlesimo during a closed practice. The incident ignited a national media frenzy, fueling the flames from the throngs of fans who were already displeased with the league's image. Since then, the details of the incident have come to light, but in the weeks and even months after the choke took place, the

Sprewell-Carlesimo "altercation" gripped the league and the mainstream media. It overshadowed a good part of the 1997–98 season, before being put to rest, for the most part, just a few months before Jordan and the Bulls took down the Utah Jazz in a wild 1998 NBA Finals.

For the NBA, "The Shot"—which, at the time, was viewed as Jordan's epochal moment—moved the focus of the league back on the court, away from the courtrooms of Sprewell and bargaining disagreements of the impending lockout.

But only for a moment.

In March 1998, arbitrator John D. Feerick, the dean of Fordham University Law School, reduced Sprewell's one-year suspension by five months and ordered that the Golden State Warriors reinstate the remainder of the All-Star swingman's four-year, $32 million contract.

"On the day I decided the Sprewell case, I remember coming from church, St. Paul's Apostle's church, across the street from campus here," Feerick told Golianopolous. "When the decision came out, the commissioner issued a press release that had negative comments about the arbitration decision."

With that, the case was closed.

"The answer is now well established," NBA commissioner David Stern said following the decision. "You cannot choke your boss and hold your job unless you play in the NBA and you are subject to arbitrator Feerick's jurisdiction."

As the 1999 season began, some four months later than it was originally scheduled, the NBA seemed, incomprehensibly, to be hanging in the balance. After a nearly twenty-year run of Bird and Magic and Jordan, the league felt void, as if it were no longer the mega show it had previously been. Something about it just felt ... off. The reputation of players was steeped in violence and reprehensible behaviors. The best team entering the season was the San Antonio Spurs, a franchise viewed from the outside as a boring and by the book: one that's gameplay failed to bring in eyeballs from casual fans. Per Golianopolous's article:

> The lockout was bad for business, both in the interim (Sports Goods Business reported that NBA-licensed sales had declined nearly 50 percent through the 1998 holiday season) and over the long term. During the lockout-shortened season, attendance was down 2 percent from 17,117 per game in 1997–98 and would not again exceed 17,000 until the 2003–04 season. Television ratings also suffered, with regular-season ratings falling from 6.3 million viewers per game during the 1997–98 NBA season to 4 million during the 2000–01 season. Ratings for the NBA Finals have never reached the heights of the Bulls-Jazz rematch from 1998 (which averaged an 18.7 rating and 29.04 million viewers), bottoming out in 2007, when the Spurs swept the Cleveland Cavaliers, a series that averaged a 6.2 rating and 9.29 million viewers.

Coming out of the lockout, the league was tasked with bringing back a fan base that was so far separated from the players on the floor in terms of salaries, it almost felt sinister. While the players' salaries were not as extravagant as they are today, the gap between athletes and the everyman was widening to levels no one had ever seen. The lockout, viewed from the outside looking in, was nothing more than millionaires going toe-to-toe with billionaires, fighting over gobs of money to which 99.9 percent of the population could not imagine making in ten lifetimes. Owners battling players was nothing new, and the results rarely worked out in the long run for all interested parties. (Major League Baseball had gone through similar suffrage in 1994, and their fate was sealed with years of poor attendance and fans that refused to look at the game the same way.)

The NBA would bounce back quicker, and in a less dramatic drop that baseball had, but it would still take time to repair the damage that had been done.

For the players involved, however, their battle seemed to work out just fine. While they would forfeit nearly half their salary that year due to missing games, the after-effect made up for it in droves. Salaries boomed to levels almost unthinkable just years prior.

Players that, under previous bylaws, would make fantastic money were now due to make the kind of money that placed them into another stratosphere.

* * *

Damon Stoudamire was a good point guard for the Portland Trail Blazers entering the 1999 season. He was mostly solid, sometimes great, and sometimes average. After returning home to Portland following a successful stint with the Toronto Raptors, who drafted him in the summer of 1996 (he went to Wilson High School, a stone's throw from where the Blazers played) the player dubbed "Mighty Mouse" for his stature and style of play had the Blazers poised to be one of the top teams in the league.

Damon was a good player. What Damon was not, however, was a max-contract kind of player. But under the new rules implemented after the lockout, that's precisely what players of his ilk saw—maximum money and contractual advantages.

"I like Damon Stoudamire. I like him as a person. I liked him as a player," Bob Whitsitt, then Trail Blazers general manager, referencing his homegrown point guard, told *The Ringer* in 2019. "But his deal was up, and he was not coming to training camp because we hadn't signed him. My owner, Paul Allen, called me and said, 'Give him the max.' I say, 'It's seven years, $86 million.' 'Yes, give him the max. Give it to him now. I want to pay him $86 million because I want him there on the first day of camp.' I'm like, 'Are you kidding me?' I like Damon, but that's not anywhere near where I would have valued Damon on the pay scale."

What Allen knew, and others were slowly coming around to, was that franchises like the Trail Blazers—well run but hardly a destination point for free agents—had to hold onto any and all assets they had, no matter the cost. And what players like Damon knew was that if there was a time to capitalize, it was after the lockout, when money was almost too easy to pass around.

The NBA needed all players, no matter their stature, on board, in uniform, ready to perform.

With no Jordan, but just a Sprewell, 50 games, and a swatch of extremely overpaid players to trot out, the NBA was ready to usher in the most tumultuous and unpredictable era in more than two decades.

The NBA that had been so predictable (in a good way) for the better part of twenty years was no more. There was Magic and Bird, and then there wasn't. There was Jordan and everyone else, and now there was just ... everyone else.

And for all of its missteps, the NBA seemed to step away from the ledge and, instead, embrace the carnival of the previous few years.

The preseason camps that took place before the shortened season have taken on almost mythical renderings, but the highlights—whether embellished or not—are glorious.

How about Master P—a rapper who had rose to fame in the middle of the decade, and who founded No Limit Records—suiting up and making his presence known almost daily at the practice facility for the Charlotte Hornets?

B. J. Armstrong, a former teammate of Jordan's who was then with the Hornets, told *The Ringer*, "He was dedicated as a player, and he was a good player—played hard, wasn't afraid, and could hit an open shot. When they played his songs in warm-ups during the games, the response of the people was incredible. I remember them chanting for him to get in the game. He brought an audience. I don't know if we should've been selling out games in the preseason."

Aside from a few gimmicky headlines (such as Master P playing a few preseason games), and watching their ratings (predictably) plummet, the season—once players found their rhythm—was enjoyable. New teams were beginning to emerge out from under the Bulls' shadow. The Blazers and Spurs staged a memorable Western Conference finals, with the Spurs winning to advance to their first NBA Finals. And, after decades of mismanagement, bad luck, and head-scratching player moves, the New York Knicks were there to meet them with a chance to bring the city its first title since 1973.

The Spurs would go on to win their first title in franchise history. Two years after they had drafted a generational power forward in Tim Duncan, the Spurs were emerging as perhaps the newest power in the league. Duncan was buoyed by future Hall of Famer David Robinson.

"You can't have a second or third or fourth without the first," Mike Budenholzer, an assistant coach on the 1999 team, told the *San Antonio Express News* in 2019. "Any time you do something for the first time, it's special. There's certainly something pretty special about '99."

The specialness of it could be summed up in everything the players and coaches had gone through in the preceding 12 months. The lockout. The uncertainty. The grueling 50 games in three months. The realization that they were ushering in the newest era of the NBA as the first champions post-Jordan.

"There were a lot of questions, obviously, with the shortened season. We knew the Lakers were going to be tough. We knew there were some challenging teams there. But we figured both Tim and I were kind of at our peaks, so it was a good time for us," says David Robinson.

Perhaps it's not surprising that the Spurs had been the last team standing. Coming into the season—whenever it was to begin—they were going to be looked on as favorites, due in large part to the continuity they had on the roster.

"It was a short training camp, but we didn't have as much work to do because we had a lot of our core guys together," said Sean Elliott. "I hadn't played much the previous two years because of knee surgeries, so I was trying to get used to playing with these guys, especially Timmy."

Timmy, a.k.a. Tim Duncan, was wise beyond his age after spending four years at Wake Forest, an almost unheard-of feat in the age of players jumping straight from high school to the pros. But he knew something special was brewing.

"Walking into that situation, I knew we had a great team and a chance to do something special," he says.

After they had secured their first title, Robinson—who had won gold as part of the Dream Team in 1992—looked around to take in the scene. He was one of the old men on the team, the torch having clearly been passed along to Duncan. But for now, it was about the moment.

Well ... for a while, at least.

"Finally accomplishing that goal, now you have to reevaluate and say, 'OK, now what are we going to do? Are we going to try to be the best and stay the best?' [But] it was more a relief than anything else. When you haven't won, people are always telling you that you don't have this, or you need that. And you never know what it is. Everyone from coaches to players get criticized, so you've kind of got to put your head down and keep plowing forward and try to figure out how to put the pieces together."

But that part was over. The Spurs had reached the mountain top in the topsy-turviest year the league had ever seen.

And leading them, venerable and snarky and unapologetically transparent, was a young(ish) head coach ready to lead them into the twenty-first century. He was, quite possibly, the most interesting coach professional sports had seen in some time, an old-school grump with new-wave views, wrapped up in a snarling, shit-eating grin that only those deep inside the Spurs organization could understand. Soon, though, the world—yes, the *whole world*—would be ready for him.

It was time to really, truly, meet Gregg Popovich.

Chapter Eight

POP GOES THE EASEL

In the state of Texas, where ghosts of gridiron past—and the promise of heroes new—often fill the gallows of adolescence, it's hard for the sport of basketball to take a foothold. It's nestled against the mystiques of Adrian Peterson and Earl Campbell; of Drew Brees and Roger Staubach; of Tom Landry and Jimmy Johnson. If football is like religion in the Deep South, Texans consider it more as a member of the family. To uproot that blood level of love takes something altogether unique and atypical. It takes a commitment to winning—and following through on that promise. But it requires a certain edge to it; to stand out in a way that pulls the crowd from their Saturday and Sunday traditions of the fall.

It requires a man with no Texas roots, but a militant, blue-collar edge.

It requires an Admiral, a Fundamental, an Argentinian, and a Frenchman, all coalescing together in splendid dysfunction and order.

It requires a once-in-a-generation talent packing it up and riding off into a (short-lived) sunset, opening the door for the aforementioned blend to succeed.

It takes the San Antonio Spurs.

* * *

Under the guidance of head coach Gregg Popovich and his long-time running mate, general manager R. C. Buford, the Spurs—thanks in large part to their five NBA championships between 1999 and 2014—are universally praised as the franchise that best utilized their scouting abilities in bringing over international talent. And it all starts with the man they affectionately call "Pop" and ends, for the most part, with raised banners in June. With an unprecedented eye for talent, a willingness to take risks and play the long game, the Spurs packed together two Hall of Fame big men (David Robinson and Tim Duncan) with the perfect collection of off-the-radar, out-of-the-blue talent they scoured the world for.

First, there was the draft—and stash—of Argentinian Manu Ginóbili.

Then, Tony Parker arrived from France.

But the mainstay, when all of those players have come and gone, is Pop. Because for all his on-court accomplishments, it's the man he is off the court that has perhaps made the biggest impact.

"I think our coaches have embraced, 'Let's get the best basketball team we can, and let's not limit ourselves by the borders of countries,'" Buford told the *New York Times* in 2013. "We're the beneficiary of the growth of basketball."

The beneficiaries, yes, but also the pioneers. While other organizations had certainly taken kindly to the idea of scouring leagues in Europe, China, Spain, and other countries (such as the Portland Trail Blazers, Atlanta Hawks, and others), it was San Antonio that proved risk-taking is almost as vital as anything. And, just as important, was their willingness to invest the resources into the process of finding those players.

"Pop and R. C. deserve a lot of credit for having the foresight to invest the time [in international scouting], and provide a lot of opportunities" for foreign players, Sam Presti, a former Spurs executive, told the *Washington Post*. "Certainly, they not only did an excellent job in identifying players, but also in creating an environment and a system where those players would want to play and would be capable of thriving."

The "environment" Presti speaks of is perhaps the most overlooked part of their success. While many people look to the talent the players brought with them—which cannot be overlooked, as Ginóbili and Parker are future Hall of Famers—it was the Spurs' willingness to be adaptable, and not the other way around, which incubated the situation. Too often when players arrive in America from overseas, they're thrust into a situation that is tailor-made for failure. A new country, where the cultures and rules are often a 180-degree turn from their roots. A language filled with colloquialisms that are both foreign and ever evolving. And basketball, the one connective tissue that, until recently, was so different from the style played in other countries that it sometimes felt like a wholly unique game.

"I was kind of amazed by how much he wanted to know about you as an individual," former player Will Perdue told *Business Week* in 2012. Other coaches, he says, stopped short of where Popovich was willing to go. "They cared about you, but they didn't really want to overextend themselves in case you got cut or got traded. . . . I don't think Pop ever even considered that. He saw you as a human being first and a basketball player second."

So when Popovich, Buford, Presti, and the rest of the Spurs organization set about dedicating their time to building the right environment for their team to thrive, it wasn't just player luxuries or an upgraded practice facility. It was more than that.

Luckily, the man in charge knew what to do. And he knew exactly how to go about getting it done.

* * *

Cured restaurant sits between Pearl Parkway and Mueller Street in downtown San Antonio. From a comfortable perch on the back balcony, you find yourself just a stone's throw from the flowing beauty of the San Antonio River, showcasing a glimpse of the tranquility that the city has to offer.

Steve McHugh is the owner and chef at Cured. Popovich is perhaps the most famous food and wine connoisseur in the state of Texas. Because of these two things, the two men have gotten to know each other quite well over the years.

Once, in 2015, before the two had become as acquainted as they are now, McHugh approached and questioned the famed coach when he spotted him struggling through an appetizer and wine pairing list. By this point in time, Popovich had won five rings, spearheaded perhaps the most translucent and muddling dynasty the sport had seen, and was just biding his time before the Hall of Fame beckoned him and many of his players. Still, here he was, brow furrowed, eyes sifting over the pages. Back and forth. Forth and back. Seeing the man known for tumultuous tantrums and sarcastic, irony-laden mid-quarter interviews were nothing new; but *this* was new.

Popovich's issues on this night were bigger than a missed call or blown assignment. Just hours before he would host the Spanish basketball officials for a dinner event—an obligation

Popovich said most coaches would pass off to assistant coaches or front office executives—the most successful coach in the NBA was in despair. Tonight, he wasn't in charge anymore. For as much as he was a wine guy, and a food guy, and a guy's guy at the same time, he now needed McHugh's help. It was much the same story as it had been a long time prior, before the dynasty, before the landmark international upheaval they would bring into the NBA.

Just over a decade prior to this night, Popovich and the Spurs hosted a contingent from Argentina in a fashion similar to this. Fine dining, proper drink, the feel of home—of family and tradition and warmth. That night, back in 2002, the correct food and wine pairing helped land one of the most important players in Spurs franchise history: Manu Ginóbili.

The environment.

"I blew 'em away, and we wined 'em, we dined 'em. We gave them photo ops. We gave 'em everything they wanted," Popovich recalled later, looking back on that night. "That's how we found out about Manu when nobody else knew about him."

The environment.

"Dinners help us have a better understanding of each individual person, which brings us closer to each other—and, on the court, understand each other better," former Spurs guard Danny Green says. On the road, whenever possible, the Spurs tend to stay over and fly out the next morning. "So, we can have that time together," former San Antonio center Pau Gasol says. "I haven't been a part of that anywhere else. And players know the importance of it as well—and how important it is to Pop."

Popovich has legendary interests outside of basketball; the rich soils of wine country is one, but it extends far beyond that. He's been regarded as the "NBA's most 'woke' coach," referring to his ability to connect with players from any and all backgrounds—black, white, Asian, Hispanic, you name it. It doesn't matter. No coach connects on a more personal level with his collective players. His time overseas, both during his military services and various coaching stints, opened his eyes to the struggles people of color face.

As Marc Spears wrote for *The Undefeated* in 2016, "Popovich also believes that many white people don't understand the stresses of being black in America. He cited having black assistant coaches talking to their children about dealing with the police, which is something he has never had to do with his two children. Popovich has also called race in America 'the elephant in the room.'"

His ability to see social issues outside the prism of his whiteness elevates his status among black players, and it's known for players coming in from other countries as well. The world scope he has, his openness with players and media alike, creates a comfort zone for people around him, which belies his gruff personality that typically flows through the TV screen. His outward appearances does not line up with the man inside.

"He's not the typical coach for sure," San Antonio Spurs forward LaMarcus Aldridge told *The Undefeated* in that same piece. "He's in tune with what is going on around the world with people and with race. He's not afraid to voice his beliefs and his opinions. He's tried to help us realize that there are more things than basketball, more than the NBA."

In the spring of 2020, amid protests around the world aligning for equality in Black communities following yet another string of harrowing and horrifying deaths at the hands of unruly police officers, Popovich, unsurprisingly, was as vocal as he's been. But perhaps at no time was he more poignant in his beliefs that he was in February 2018, when, off the cuff, he regaled the gathered media with the following:

I think it's pretty obvious. The league is made up of a lot of black guys. To honor that and understand it is pretty simplistic. How would you ignore that? But more importantly, we live in a racist country that hasn't figured it out yet. And it's always important to bring attention to it, even if it angers some people. The point is, you have to keep it in front of everybody's nose so they understand it still hasn't been taken care of and we have a lot of work to do. It's a remembrance and a bit of a celebration in some ways. It sounds odd because we're not there yet, but it's always important to remember what has passed and what is being experienced now by the black population. It's a celebration of some of the good things that have happened and a reminder that there's a lot more work to do.

*　＊　＊＊*

Gregg Popovich was born in East Chicago, Illinois, a small shipping canal town most famous for blues legend Catfish Keith, former major-league baseball player Kenny Lofton, and, now, himself. The Inland Steel Company had been the main source of stable work for families for 105 years before it shut down in 1998. Every day, mothers, fathers, uncles, aunts, brothers, and sisters awoke early, packed their rusty lunch pails, and headed for Inland, feeling blessed for continuous work and wanting nothing more.

Sunnyside, the neighborhood where Popovich was born, was known for its curvilinear street grid, suburban vibe, and that fact that nearly 90 percent of its citizens were either black or Hispanic.

It was also ranked as the safest neighborhood in all of East Chicago, flying in the face of racial stereotypes. In that sector, Popovich was privy to an upbringing of strong, mixed relations, where the color of your skin or the background of your genes meant less than the generosity in your smile or the authenticity of your handshake.

In the late 1800s, East Chicago was nothing more than inhibited swampland. It wasn't until the early 1900s before the town built itself from the literal ground up. Swamp creatures gave way to human beings from all over the globe, all seeking the same fate: solid work, solid families, solid living

Popovich's father was Serbian, his mother Croatian; growing up in this small town (where the population has never crested over 30,000 people), there was no, "Don't go there," "Stay away from this place if you like this or that." Kids and adults alike roamed the streets, the shops, the restaurants, all uninhibited by economic or racial limitations.

"It's easier for white people because we haven't lived that experience. It's difficult for many white people to understand the day-to-day feeling that many black people have to deal with," Popovich told Marc Spears in his article from *The Undefeated.* "I didn't talk to my kids about how to act in front of a policeman when you get stopped. I didn't have to do that. All of my black friends have done that. There's something that's wrong about that, and we all know that."

That Popovich found a pocket of the country where he could dine among folks of wildly different backgrounds was something of a minor miracle. All throughout states such as Indiana, Missouri, Illinois, etc., during the formative years when children are at their most vulnerable and perceptive—the Midwest was embattled with what was known as "sundown towns"—towns where, black Americans knew, they were not welcome once the sun went down.

"I grew up in an integrated area. Everyone had jobs in the steel mill. There was a Puerto Rican family, a black family and a Czechoslovakian family, a Serbian family, whatever. Everybody was fine because everybody had a job. It kind of does boil down to that. "

Unburdened by the realities of visualized segregation—a rarity in this Midwest part of the country in the 1950s and 1960s, to be sure—the man who would facilitate and build the most diverse franchise in basketball was raised knowing that your skin color meant nothing to your character or your abilities. To him, everyone, no matter their background or upbringing, was equal.

"I don't think you can understand his success without (believing in) that," Steven Koblik, then a history professor at Pomona who served as an academic adviser to the team, told *Grantland* in 2012. "This is a working-class kid who long ago discovered that what he didn't have in natural talent he could make up just by outworking people. No one questions how much film he watches. No one questions his game plan," Robinson says. "He does his work."

And because of that strong belief, whether it's relating to his black players, or French, or Spanish, or Turkish, Popovich has never lost sight of the struggles faced by minorities.

"If you're disenfranchised, you got no job, you got no hope, you got nothing, bad things are going to start to happen. It's not just America, it's all over the world. Maybe that's where I started to be aware of things. Relationships with people are what it's all about. You have to make players realize you care about them."

It's a notion he has carried with him from the salt-of-the-earth roads of East Chicago, south to San Antonio, and directly into his teachings.

* * *

When LaMarcus Aldridge became one of the most sought-after free agents in the league after the 2015 season, the lanky former

University of Texas power forward was faced with, essentially, two top options: remain with the Portland Trail Blazers, the franchise that had drafted him nine seasons prior; or head back home to Texas and join the Spurs, igniting life into what appeared to be a declining era. Tim Duncan was on his last legs. Ginóbili and Tony Parker were still effective, but their play had dropped considerably. All three were staring down the barrel of retirement.

Portland carried its share of appeal. So, too, did the pull of home. In the end, Aldridge strapped on his saddle and headed Southeast. The family waited, and so, too, did an enigma of a coach whom the forward needed to experience.

As it turned out, art and new experiences formed a bond between the pair.

Popovich's ability to turn his message into actions is legendary, and it wasn't long before Aldridge experienced that firsthand. When the Spurs took a trip to New York during Aldridge's first season in San Antonio, the cultured coach took his multicultural club to see the most cultured of plays Broadway had ever seen— Lin-Manuel Miranda's *Hamilton*, which famously employed a largely diverse cast. Many players had never been to Broadway; to have their first time be with their white coach, to a play outlining how immigrants from widely differentiating backgrounds can come together, was more than symbolic: it was genius.

Aldridge said the "color-blind" Popovich tries to keep his players "intrigued every day" by asking them questions about the world. Aldridge also added that one example of how Popovich can relate well to people of color was his strong relationship with ex-Spurs forward Stephen Jackson, who grew up amid violence and poverty while being raised by a single mother in Port Arthur, Texas.

"When you get to know him, color doesn't matter to him," Aldridge said about Popovich. "He can relate. People can say that he and Stephen Jackson are really close. Stephen Jackson is the opposite of being from Europe. It doesn't matter what you are. He connects with all people . . . He's so open-minded to everything. There is a big world out there and a whole lot of stuff going on."

Being able to have open conversations about subjects that are often taboo in locker rooms—especially from coaches, an alarming amount of whom are still white—softens the natural barrier that coaches and players sometimes face on these real-world issues.

"It's pretty obvious that the national stain of slavery continues to permeate our social system in this country," Popovich told Spears. "People want to ignore it, don't want to talk about it, because it's inconvenient. And when I saw *Birth of a Nation* when Tony brought it to San Antonio, I thought it was a great way to slap people right straight in the face. Not just say, 'That slavery thing. There were probably cotton fields, it's kind of hard.' It was hard and disgusting and humiliating and life-defeating.

"It shows it in that film. It's not just the physical stuff. It's the mental, daily degradation that people suffered. It pervades families, psyches. To this day, we see the precipitant of all that."

* * *

Perhaps where Popovich shines most in connecting to his players is by keeping the basketball in perspective: it's a game, and nothing more.

"If there's one thing he took from the whole experience, maybe it was to see basketball players as more than athletes," Mike Blitz, a former player from Saratoga, California, who was coached by Popovich at Pomona-Pitzer, told *Grantland* in 2015. "He viewed us as people who have something to say."

Popovich's coaching career took a few odd twists and turns, but perhaps it's his time at Pomona-Pitzer—part of a collection of five schools that now fall under the Claremont Colleges umbrella—that best describes who Popovich is as a person and a leader. During his decade-long run in Claremont, California, he not only became ingrained in the culture, but, more so, showcased a vastly different style and persona than his players were used to seeing. He showed them a world outside of their mostly cushy upbringings and upper-middle class lifestyles.[9] "Coaching at Pomona didn't make him see us as human beings," Dave DiCesaris, one of Popovich's players at Pomona-Pitzer. "He already had that curiosity about people. That's just what made him and Pomona a perfect fit."

Popovich had joined Pomona-Pitzer after a stint coaching the US Air Force Academy; in that time, he also attended the University of Denver, where he earned his master's in physical education and sports science. Before that, he had served five years of required active duty in the United States Air Force, where he toured Eastern Europe and the Soviet Union with the US Armed Forces Basketball Team.

As Baxter Holmes wrote for ESPN in 2019, when describing the eccentricities of Popovich:

> Over the past few decades, Popovich has sliced a culinary trail across America—one curated in private, if not in secret. He's patronized the finest restaurants, spent millions of dollars, left countless four-figure tips, turned himself into a first-order oenophile. He forged fast friendships with the nation's premier gourmands. And all to a singular purpose. As one source close to Popovich says, "It's a passion for him, but it's also a tool."

---

9   In 2007, CNN ranked Claremont as the fifth-best place to live in the United States, and top locale in California.

That outgoing, worldly view was a key cog in helping the Spurs navigate the potentially choppy waters of not only bringing in an influx of players from outside the United States who spoke little English and were far removed from their families, but for guys who were coming in to take other players' jobs. Immediately.

It's also been evident in how he connects them, as worldly issues infiltrate the locker room.

Case in point: when Colin Kaepernick made national headlines during the 2016 football season by kneeling during the national anthem to protest police brutality against black and other minority citizens, stirring up waves on the right, left, and middle of the political world, the potential for divisions in the locker rooms—across all sports—was palpable. It became a race issue, a political issue, and a socioeconomic issue.

"A pretty good group of people immediately thought he was disrespecting the military," Popovich said to Holmes. "That had nothing to do with his protest. In fact, he was able to do what he did because of what the military does for us. Most thinking people understand that, but there is always going to be an element that wants to jump on a bandwagon and that's what is unfortunate about our country. The military, obviously, is as equal as they can be. I also traveled with USA Basketball teams. I saw cultures and players in every place. I guess it just stuck. When we started getting foreign players, the more socially conscious they were, the more they would talk, the more they would interact and feel responsible for one another and owe each other something. It just felt natural."

Popovich is perhaps the "worldliest" coach in the NBA. He majored in Soviet studies at the Air Force Academy. He speaks Russian and Serbian. His playing experience was with the military basketball teams during his stint in the armed forces, where he traveled all over Eastern Europe in the 1970s. When he joined the Spurs as an assistant coach in 1988, Popovich traveled to see the European championships in Cologne, where he was only one of two NBA coaches present. The other? Don Nelson.

Popovich bristled at the preponderance of people who said international players didn't defend, that they wouldn't socialize or adapt to the American culture, that they wouldn't learn English, they weren't strong dribblers, they couldn't handle a reduced role, or that they played a soft brand of basketball. "I thought that was really ignorant," Pop says. "I couldn't believe that it was a pool that wasn't being used."

Popovich has been quoted as saying foreign-born kids are "fundamentally harder working than most American kids," and that the Spurs wanted to avoid the trap so many of their fellow NBA teams were falling under, which was the end of the road for the developmental habits that are built in the less-structured environment in the US.

As Seth Wickersham of ESPN wrote:

> Most of the foreign players not only have more experience playing basketball but more experience playing an unself-ish style, with lots of passing and motion and screens, as messy as it is pure. As Spurs director of basketball operations Sean Marks, a New Zealander who played for San Antonio for two seasons, puts it, "The ball doesn't stick." For better or worse, the ball often sticks in America. A few months ago, Pop was scouting an opponent. He won't say which one. On video, Pop saw an international player wide open for a shot, with a confused look on his face. That's because his point guard, an American, was drib-bling in circles. "It has to be a really different experience for him," Pop says, laughing. "Where am I? Is this a differ-ent game? Is it a different sport?"

As Popovich has noted, when speaking of international players, they " . . . have less. They appreciate things more. And they're very coachable."

He's also, as Ginolbli bluntly puts it . . . real.

"He can be an asshole on the court," Ginóbili says. "But when the game is over, you know he is just doing his job."

Of course, it's much easier when his best player, Duncan, who was raised in the Virgin Islands and learned the game by playing point guard in pickup games on a rugged outdoor court, is best known for putting team first; when Parker, raised in France, is okay trading stats for wins; when Ginóbili, raised in Argentina, is fine coming off the bench. And the Spurs have whiffed on imports (Luis Scola) and scored with Americans (Kawhi Leonard). Still, there's a different vibe in the Spurs facility, as if deplaning in a foreign airport.

Chapter Nine

FOREIGN-LED DYNASTY, AMERICANIZED

Before he was known as the five-time NBA championship–winning coach; before his halftime and end-of-quarter TV segments cemented him into legendary meme status; and before he was known as the "Master of Foreign Scouting," Gregg Popovich was known simply as Popo.

An Army veteran, Popovich had cut his teeth with the US Air Force before going on to be the head coach of the small community college Pomona-Pitzer, where he led the school to their first outright title in sixty-eight years. While at Pomona, Popovich struck up a friendship with the legendary Larry Brown, who was, at the time, the head coach at Kansas.

Popovich joined Pomona-Pitzer in 1979; he took the season off in 1985 to join Brown's staff at Kansas as a "volunteer assistant," where he soaked up as much knowledge from the seasoned coach as he could.

"He [Popovich] wasn't doing a lot down there," Brown told Mike Monroe of the *San Antonio Express* in 2014. "I told him to come stay with me at Kansas and he ended up spending the year with me there. He sat on the bench and was a big part of our program."

Brown welcomed Popovich's input from the moment he stepped on campus, treating him like the rest of his assistants. "He was respectful," Brown said. "Everybody is respectful of the head coach, and especially coming from where he was coming from. But we spent so much time together and there was a lot of exchange of ideas and it was easy to see he has qualities that make him special.

"My whole thing is I can teach anybody all the basketball I was taught, but you can't teach loyalty. I always tell guys I can't teach them to love me, so if they care about me that's really important. I just loved him as a person. I respected his knowledge, obviously, but he's also one of the most decent, loyal guys I've ever been around, and I just wanted to be connected."

After a year under the tutelage of Brown, Popovich returned to Pomona-Pitzer.

That season, his squad received a nice treat, in the form of an athletic beatdown, but an unforgettable experience nonetheless: They would travel to Lawrence, Kansas, to face the Jayhawks. Popovich would take on his mentor in perhaps the most lopsided contest ever played, from a talent standpoint.

Before tipoff at the famous Allen Fieldhouse in Lawrence, Kansas, on December 1, 1987, some Pomona-Pitzer Sagehens took photos of themselves in one of college basketball's most storied arenas. A few of the players even asked Jayhawks star Danny Manning, the soon-to-be NCAA Player of the Year and No. 1 overall NBA draft pick, to pose with them.

"Enjoy this experience," Brown told the Sagehens team before the game as he came to visit Popovich. "This is going to be better than anything else you experience as college players. Now, we're going to kick your ass so don't even worry about that. Just make sure you enjoy yourselves."

After Brown left, and after the beatdown that did occur, he invited Popovich to join his staff to Kansas after the season. But plans would change, as Brown was hired by the San Antonio Spurs. Popovich saddled up with Brown, and the two headed to Texas.

* * *

Popovich, Brown, and an all-star staff—including R. C. Buford, Alvin Gentry, and Ed Manning—arrived in San Antonio in 1988, and Popovich instantly became the coach's top assistant. That was, until the entire staff was fired by owner Red McCombs in 1992. After the housecleaning, Popovich moved west and joined the Golden State Warriors for a brief stint in 1992, where he learned as an assistant under future Hall of Fame head coach Don Nelson. He returned to the Spurs a couple of years later as the franchise's general manager and vice president of basketball operations.

Then, two years later, in 1996, Popovich's world—as well as that of the Spurs organization—would be flipped on its ear.

That season had been an unrelenting nightmare for the Spurs. Their transcendent star, David Robinson, had missed all but six games after initially hurting his back in the preseason, then breaking his foot shortly after returning in December. Losing their star player brought forth a trickle-down effect, one that would ultimately lead to one of the top dynasties the NBA has ever seen. The first domino to fall was head coach Bob Hill, who was let go just 18 games into his third season (with the team at 3–15).

"We have perceived over some period of time now that the team has not been playing anywhere near as competitively as it should," Jack Diller, then the Spurs' vice president, told the assembled media. "We had dropped to a point where it was unacceptable."

Although losing Robinson had proven to be the final straw in Hill's tenure with the Spurs, there was another entity lurking in the background which ultimately led to the decision to let him go. From his spot high atop the Alamodome, Popovich had been watching, waiting, studying the team and the league. After decades of head coaching stints in small colleges, and riding shotgun next to coaches like Brown and Nelson—and now learning the nuances of player evaluations and drafting—the growing sentiment in the organization was that the best head coach in the building was not Hill, but in fact the man watching over him.

"It was more than David [Robinson]," Hill would later tell the San Antonio TV station KSAT-TV. "It was a process of trying to play one way and practice another in anticipation of David coming back, so it was difficult for everybody. We were outmanned every single night. We've finally built a terrific foundation for winning, and my only regret is that I won't be able to be a part of the finishing touches."

Popovich would take over officially from Hill 19 games into the season, with the club already 12 games under .500. On top of Robinson, the Spurs would be without sharpshooting guard Chuck Person for the season due to an injury and Sean Elliott, arguably the team's second-best player at the time, would be limited throughout the year. It was one of those snakebitten years that's hard to describe unless you've lived through it, but the 20-win campaign would yield immediate results: the first was Popovich. The second, coming in June of 1997, was an almost supernatural talent from Wake Forest by the name of Tim Duncan.

* * *

For Duncan, his career seemed almost certain to start in Boston as opposed to with the Spurs. Ahead of the 1997 draft, the Boston Celtics had a 27.5 percent chance of landing the coveted first spot in the draft. Given the odds, and the franchise's place in NBA lore, it seemed almost predestined.

"I was back in college and at a friend's house watching the [draft] lottery," Duncan recalled. "I was pretty sure I was coming to Boston. They had the two picks. Then the sixth pick went by and the third pick went by, both to Boston, and, all of a sudden, I kinda had a renewed interest in what was going on. Then Philly came up—and then I knew I was going to San Antonio and that was a great feeling. I was looking forward to going to the NBA. I had waited four years. I didn't know what to expect. I just knew I was going to play."

The following month, just 83 miles from where he had dominated the world of college basketball, the 1997 NBA Draft arrived, and the "Big Fundamental," as he would be known, was officially on his way to the Lone Star State. When David Stern announced the pick, TNT's Ernie Johnson quipped that "Tim Duncan has some fans up here in the Carolinas." The crowd erupted as if he were staying to play for the hometown Hornets.

But he wasn't. Duncan was on his way to join the Admiral, David Robinson.

Seventeen years later, Popovich is a future Hall of Fame coach with five NBA titles.

Hill has lived in San Antonio for the past eleven years and has spent several years coaching in China, Taiwan, and Japan.

"It's part of life—[Popovich] always wanted to be the head coach, I just didn't recognize it quick enough," Hill said.

Two seasons later, the Spurs would win their first title in franchise history, topping the Knicks in five games in an NBA Finals berated by fans. The two teams were plodding, porous offensively, bruising on defense, and, quite generally, boring. But the results were in: Popovich, after casting Hill aside, was the clear man in charge. And Duncan was a budding superstar.

But the Spurs faced an old foe in victory, one that has yet to be dispelled: Father Time.

Robinson was thirty-three years of age and had already spent a decade in the league. Clearly, he was no longer the player he once was. Mario Elie was thirty-six; Elliott, thirty. Most of the roster, while still able-bodied, were born in the 1960s. Some, like Jerome Kersey, were in the twilight of their careers. Others, like Will Perdue, Steve Kerr, and Avery Johnson, we're knocking on the door.

For the Spurs to continue to capitalize on their hot-shot coach and Duncan, retooling the roster was a must. They had to get younger, sure, but they would have to be good . . . and be creative in doing so. Winning teams are not rewarded with high draft picks in the NBA; the Spurs—playing in one of the smaller markets, from an NBA standpoint, therefore having to be creative in how they construct their roster—would be contenders every year, thus always picking near the bottom of the draft. Popovich and R. C. Buford, who had now taken over general manager duties, would have to scour the globe for talent, for guys under-the-radar that other teams refused to believe in, or who simply had yet to be discovered.

* * *

"Who did we just pick?"

Tim Duncan was confused. And, truthfully you couldn't blame him. It was the summer of 1999, and the Spurs had just polished off their first title in franchise history. While players were scattered about the beaches of Cabo, the Bahamas, and Miami, the coaching staff and personnel department had been hard at work—as were every other team in the league—preparing to draft the next installments to their rosters.

San Antonio had the 29th pick of the first round, choosing Leon Smith. They then immediately traded him to the Dallas Mavericks, leaving their second-round pick (57th overall) as their final chance to improve the roster through the draft.

And one by one, players from the usual collegiate hotspots were taken.

A. J. Bramlett, Arizona.
Ryan Robertson, Kansas.
J. R. Koch, Iowa.

Player after player, NBA washout after NBA washout, were meticulously picked off the board. GMs scurried off to speak to their local media, ensuring that they got the guys they targeted, the ones that would propel them to the next phase.

They lied. All of them. The lone man to tell the truth would be R. C. Buford, Gregg Popovich, or anyone else from the Spurs organization who claimed to have gotten the pick correct that night. And although it would take three full seasons before he would make his way from the Viola Reggio Calabria squad selected out of Italy, the Argentinian they selected would prove to be more than worth the wait. And although almost no one outside of the Spurs organization had heard of him before that night, it wouldn't take long before the Spurs' vision was soon realized.

Fifty-seven picks into the night, with just Eddie Lucas of Virginia Tech to follow, the Spurs added the first of their legendary pull from the globe in Manu Ginóbili.[10]

Two years later, in 2001, the second piece of that puzzle would come into play.

With the 28th pick in that year's draft, the Spurs took a diminutive guard from France by the name of Tony Parker.

* * *

"I just remember how excited R. C. was after it worked out in the draft," Sam Presti told Sam Amick of *USA Today*. "The draft is a different animal, so you never know how the board will ultimately work or fall. There was some uneasiness about whether or not he [Parker] would be available at our pick."

It didn't take long for the Spurs to realize their investment in the Frenchman was worth it. Although just nineteen years of age, Parker fit in almost immediately with his teammates. His combination of speed, the shiftiness, and the shot making all added up to equal a player who played well above his age.

* * *

It was just five months before he was handed the reins to the franchise, and just two years removed from their first title, with a veteran-laden backcourt. In that, Popovich could have been threatening the harmony inside the locker room. The young Frenchman—handsome, suave, cocky—seemingly taking the

---

10 Of the 58 players drafted in 1999, Manu Ginóbili was one of only five to appear in more than 1,000 games, and the only one taken in the second round to appear in at least 500 games.

point guard job from veterans Terry Porter (twenty years his senior) and Jason Hart. Out the door from the previous year were respected players such as Avery Johnson and Steve Kerr. All signs pointed to the job—seemingly overnight—being given to Parker.

"He came into a difficult situation," Buford said of Parker. "He was handed the ball as a 19-year-old [and told to] go run a team that had two future Hall of Famers [Duncan and David Robinson]. He [was] trying to grow into a leadership role . . . and you've got a coach who's very demanding, a system that's pretty sophisticated . . . . That wouldn't have been easy."

Parker, who retired after the 2018–19 season, looks back on those initial first years with a humbleness that doesn't add up to the stat sheet, when he averaged 9.2 points, 4.3 assists, and 2.6 rebounds as a rookie.

"My first three or four years, it was definitely tough coming from France, a different country and [Popovich] wanted me to grow fast," Parker told NBA TV in 2013, via *USA Today*. "Sometimes I had a hard time because I felt like he was never happy, that he is a hard coach to please. But when I look back at it, he made me very strong mentally and now I really appreciate all those moments and the growing pains."

As would play out over the two decades that followed, it was Popovich who calmed the waters internally. In the nineteen-year-old, Popovich saw a child—a talented one, but a child. One that needed to be handled differently than other players on the roster. His ability to diagnose Parker, and the rest of the team, was just a small sample of his gift.

"Popovich is great off the court, always helping us out," Parker told *The Undefeated*. "Of course, take your job seriously. But he tries to keep us focused on that this isn't the only thing we have to live on. There is a bigger picture to focus on and think about. I never had a coach who really tried to help you think about things outside of basketball. That's really what he does. He tries to get you better at the game of basketball while also learning about what's going on day-to-day."

While Ginóbili was the first international player Popovich picked who had not attended college in the United States, Parker was his first opportunity to show players coming over that his style was just … unique. He understood their pasts; he understood the challenges they would face upon arrival, such as the language barriers, and that the normally short leash you gave to younger players wouldn't work. "I think the overall relationship with Pop shows a great deal of growth from Tony," Buford said. "There's a lot of the time when Pop sits there and lets Tony run the group. And if you look in the huddles, there's times when Tony sits down in the timeouts and takes over the huddle. I just think the respect that he's earned from everybody is really evident."

Parker's tenure with the Spurs would end after the 2018 season—he would play one year for the Charlotte Hornets before retiring—and those inside the building still revere him for all he brought to the franchise.

"I'm happy for him on a personal level," said Presti. "He's put in a lot of hard work and has overcome plenty of peaks and valleys—as any great player has to. I think I can certainly tell you that our team has a very, very deep respect for him not only on the floor but also his role within that evolution of that team and their sustained excellence."

* * *

Three years after being drafted, Ginóbili was twenty-five years old when he first donned the white, silver, and black Spurs jersey. And it didn't take long for the home crowd, during an otherwise sleepy preseason game against the Philadelphia 76ers, to see why the hype had been building steadily since he was drafted way back in 1999. He scored 9 points on 3-of-5 shooting; he hustled down rebounds that he had no business getting; and he threw pinpoint passes through traffic, at eye-popping angles, with effortless flicks of the wrist.

When the Spurs played their final preseason game in front of their home crowd, the buzz in the air that night was not about the unfettered thoughts of the upcoming season. Sure, the Spurs were expected to be good—really good, if all broke right—but that was the expectation every season. No, this night was about the Argentinian import, and the truly exotic style of play he was bringing to the table.

And he had been preparing for this since long before the NBA, or the Spurs, or Popovich were even a glint in his eye.

"He would go to the basket, get crushed, stand up to shoot free throws, and get crushed all over again," Pepe Sanchez, a childhood friend of Ginóbili who won gold with Argentina in 2004, told ESPN's Zach Lowe in 2018. "He was so tiny. He was fragile." Sanchez and Ginóbili had waged battles big and small in their youth, through the circuits and into the professional ranks in Argentina.

As a kid, Ginóbili's father gave him special glasses with frames that flipped down, parallel to the floor, so Ginóbili couldn't see where he was dribbling. He outfitted him with gloves that eliminated the sensation of touch on the palms, forcing Ginóbili to manipulate the ball with his fingertips. "I was four, dribbling around the kitchen wearing all this stuff," Ginóbili chuckled later at the memory. "I was an experiment."

It was known early on that Ginóbili possessed something different when the basketball graced his left hand. He had an ability to see the game in ways others around him could only dream of. And although he was spindly and gangly and awkward, his eyes and brain often lent himself to be more of an asset on the floor throughout his youth. His body would take time, but everything else about him was ready for the big time.

As Lowe wrote:

> When Ginóbili's body caught up with his brain, he jumped from the local to national radar—barely. He made Argentina's under-22 team in 1996 only because several players above him had scheduling conflicts.
>
> "He was nothing special," said Andrés Nocioni, who teamed with Ginóbili to win the 2004 gold medal at the Summer Olympics. "But you could see he moved differently than normal people. Like a snake."

Before his arrival in 2002, his future teammates knew little of the player who would become as synonymous with the franchise as any player in team history. "I told Timmy [Duncan], 'This guy is coming, and nobody in the U.S. knows how good he is.' And Timmy gave me that whole raised eyebrow thing he does," said Popovich.

But as confident as Pop was, and no matter how the team's PR staff could spin the narrative around his arrival, Ginóbili was still arriving slight of frame, with zero NBA experience. He was listed at 6-foot-6—that part looked accurate—and 202 pounds. The latter, however, looked anything but.

"I was honestly scared and afraid for how he would hold up over time," Popovich said. "I get chills thinking about it now."

He would make an immediate splash—in the season opener against the defending champion Lakers, Ginóbili scored 7 points, recorded 4 steals, and had 3 assists and 2 rebounds in just under 20 minutes in the Spurs' win. But as would prove to be the case for the rest of his career, it was the way he did all of the little things that differentiated him from almost every other player in the league. He struggled at times with the stylistic differences of the NBA (and especially the Spurs)—"I was so frustrated that first year, waiting in the corner, I wanted the ball, to make decisions. I was 25, and I wanted to take the world by storm. I thought I knew everything."—but he adapted quickly, and by the end of the season was a key cog in the Spurs' attack. His numbers weren't astronomical—7.6 points, 2.3 rebounds, and 2.0 assists per game in 20 minutes—but he was finding his groove.

"He just gave himself permission to play how he wanted," Duncan told Lowe in 2018, a big laugh tumbling out of his mouth. "He beat us into submission. Pop would be pulling his hair out, but eventually, we all saw Manu was steps ahead of everyone else."

Once the rest of the club figured out how to play alongside a unique talent like Ginóbili, the rest, as they say, is history. Parker and Ginóbili—along with future teammates such as Boris Diaw (France), Tiago Splitter (Brazil), Patty Mills (Australia), and hosts of other international talent—would form the nucleus of four more championships for the Spurs before the big three of Parker, Ginóbili, and Duncan all sailed away into retirement.

"When it comes to the Spurs and international players, a lot of the focus is often on Manu Ginóbili and Tony Parker, and rightfully so—for a while they were two of the best international players who had ever played in the NBA," Garrett Jochnau wrote for *Bleacher Report* in 2013. "But I think what makes the Spurs unique is the way they dipped overseas for a bunch of talent and filled out the roster for some of those role players. In 2014, that was kind of the cusp of when we really saw an emergence of international play. If you look at the guys from that team it was Parker, Ginóbili, Kawhi…but you also had to fill it out. Boris Diaw, Patty Mills was incredible, [Marco] Belinelli, Aaron Baynes."

Jochnau continued in his praise of the Spurs, and their influence in growing the NBA into a league that has embraced international players.

"Coming off that 2014 season [the Spurs' final title], you saw a big spike in international players. 2015 was the first time you saw higher than 10 percent of the rosters being international players. A lot of that was people saw what was happening in San Antonio. They were so much more than the Big Three; they had a roster built for their system. Obviously Golden State built a very impressive roster that was unique and will not be replicated anytime soon, but their style of play was very much a resemblance of San Antonio. Move the ball fast. Three-point heavy. None of that happens without Duncan, obviously. He was a revolutionary player, and I think the best player of the decade. But what made San Antonio great for so many years was their ability to develop players and not have to chase big-money players. They were very much finding their guys at the end of the first round, early second. But they were also investing in guys like Splitter who didn't come over immediately, but when he did was very productive for them."

Their style went beyond simply watching players and taking risks here and there. Popovich and Buford were instrumental in the investment to make sure the Spurs were ahead of the game when it came to scouting those players and leagues.

San Antonio was the trendsetter for the league in this department. As John Walters of *Newsweek* wrote in 2014, the Spurs not only talked the talk in their views of international players, but, as technology continued to progress and scouting became more of a focal point, enabling them to see and discover more and more players, they ultimately walked the walk: On opening night of the NBA's 2013–14 season, the Spurs made history by having 10 foreign-born players on the roster. Meanwhile, San Antonio's opponent for the NBA Finals that season (and the previous), the world champion Miami Heat, were one of two NBA franchises (the Philadelphia 76ers were the other) that had no international players on their entire roster.

"San Antonio—the market, the coach, the franchise itself—creates this very unique incubator for talent," Ben Golliver, who covered the Portland Trail Blazers for years before working for the *Washington Post*, told me. "Their thought was always, 'We just want to get the best players, with most upside, here, regardless of whatever. We're confident that once we get them here, it's almost like an academy, and we're going to be able to teach them the 'Spurs Way.' Oh, and they also had Tim Duncan." If you look at the makeup of their team, they have coaches with international voices. They have a female coach in Becky Hammon. That diversity of opinion, and that culture, makes you more open to envisioning players from a country who may never have come to America before and had success. It makes you open to the idea of 'Hey, this could work.'"

The league is still American born, and American bred; thanks to the Spurs, and a whole contingency of teams that are following suit, the lines are blurred.

Chapter Ten

THE WORLD'S GAME?

Mens sana in corpore sano

⚒

A healthy mind in a perfect body

—Latin phrase

High atop the Parthenon, on the Athenian Acropolis, Greece, the columnis-temple which is dedicated to the goddess Athena— whom the people of Athens considered their patron saint—the multi-columned temple is engraved with the perfect metaphor for the 2004 Olympics. From around the globe, perfect athletes, wrapped in perfect casings, descended upon the perfectly set small island bordering southeast of Albania, steeling themselves for the world's oldest and most decorated test of athletic expression.

It had been 108 years since the Olympics kicked into their final form, having evolved from the Games of the I Olympiad; Athens, fittingly, had been the birthright all of those years prior. Returning to its place of origin, the 2004 Olympics figured to evolve much as the previous three had: the Chinese would dominate on the mats in gymnastics; Jamaica would excel in track and field; and the United States would roll out their army of professional assassins to the basketball court, and take the gold home just as they had done every time since the initial Dream Team back in 1992. They would roll through the medal count, leaving every other nation in their wake.

When the 2004 Olympics wrapped up on August 29, 2004, some of the predictions came to reality; the Americans did, in fact, mop up at the medal table, tallying 101 total medals, including 36 gold. The next closest competitor, Russia, received 90 medals.

A total of 10,625 athletes from 201 countries descended into Athens with visions of rising to the top of their sport, laying claim to the title of "Best in the World." The scope of the games was, as usual, worldwide. With the breathtaking landscapes of Greece dotting the background, the games did as they do every four years: unite the world—if for only one month—in athletic competitions, reminding us all that commonality can be a glorious thing.

One of the big predictions that fell flat in a defiant, humbling manner involved the United States, basketball, and the universal view of their place in the pantheon of the sport. Because for one summer (at least), it became apparent—*painfully* apparent— that the world had not only caught up to what the United States was about, but had—for this year, at least—surpassed them with stunning ease.

The downfall began months ahead of the games, but only became noticeable when the United States arrived in Greece.

Some players said the right things:

"My whole time in Greece depends on one thing," Richard Jefferson, a forward for the United States, said upon arrival. "I'm not here to be an ambassador. I'm not here to see sights or travel around. I'm here to try and win a gold medal."

Most players, however, went to Greece seeking paradise: big waves, big sun, and big cocktails. And unlike that celebrated 1992 roster, which averaged twenty-seven years of age (and was skewed heavily by the lone college player, Christian Laettner, who was twenty-two years of age and scarcely played), the 2004 roster was practically delivered to Greece in a stroller: the average age was just twenty-four years. Two of the players (Carmelo Anthony and LeBron James) were not yet legally able to drink. Four more (Dwyane Wade, Carlos Boozer, Amar'e Stoudemire, and Emeka Okafor) were either twenty-one or twenty-two years old.

"I was talking to one of the Puerto Rican players—he was forty years old!" Chuck Daly, who went to Greece merely as a visitor after coaching the 1992 squad, told *GQ* years later for a piece titled "Dunk'd: An Oral History of the 2004 Dream Team."

"Plus, he could play! We are now playing boys against men. Maybe four [players on the 2004 Olympic team] should have still been in college. And some in high school."

Age alone does not mean the team was bereft of talent; far from it, in fact, when you break down the roster. James will go down as one of the game's all-time greats. Both Tim Duncan and Allen Iverson are already enshrined in the Hall of Fame, with no doubt that Anthony and Wade will be joining them shortly.

No, this version of Team USA didn't lack talent. What they lacked was something far more damaging, and far more insulting to the confidence and belief that the United States had carried with them so well in years past:

This team lacked intimidation.

Where the 1992 Dream Team would enter a room with the game won already, based simply off the intimidation they forecasted on their opponents, this team walked into the arena and the collective breath from the other teams in the tournament was, simply...*meh*.

And it was never more apparent than in the opening game on August 15, when they belly flopped against Puerto Rico, 92–73. It should also be made clear that the Puerto Rican squad which featured one—*ONE*—NBA player, Carlos Arroyo. To put the loss into further context, the commonwealth went 3–4 that summer, finishing sixth overall.

"The first half, we ended up by 22 points. If we were on the other side, we would be frustrated, too. We made history that night," Arroyo said.

Those in attendance were flabbergasted at the display Team USA was putting on. This wasn't the powerhouse Soviet Union or Croatian teams of years past; hell, this wasn't even Argentina, one of the team's most thought *might* give this iteration of Team USA fits.

"I [remember saying] I can't understand why they are so bad. Why are they so bad?" said Carsten Mayer, a reporter from the German paper *Stuttgarter Nachrichten*.

But on that night, they were, and it was clear that the warts shown were there to stay.

"[After the game] Tim Duncan shook my hand and said we deserved to win," said José Ortiz, a center for Puerto Rico. "Nobody else shook my hand. Eight years ago, we would have been taking pictures with the U.S.A. players. Now we are beating them."

"After that, I think teams stopped being intimidated. It was almost like Rocky hitting Drago over the left eye and Rocky's trainer saying, "See? He's just a man!" said Tom Tolbert, who was calling the game for ESPN.

After the game, Arroyo turned and headed toward the exits, with still over a minute left in the game. He tugged at the "Puerto

Rico" on the front of his jersey, sending a direct message to not just the United States, but to the world at large: USA's reign of terror was over.

"You could have sent the [NBA expansion team Charlotte] Bobcats, who've never played, and you should have won this championship," Peter Vecsey told *Bleacher Report* in 2010. "Come on! It's a joke! Puerto Rico. Who'd they have?"

The loss stung, yet it did little to hurt their gold medal chances; it was, however, far more damaging to their confidence. And it was evident from that night onward that Team USA was far, far removed from the Dream Team that had blown through the 1992 games. Everything the 2004 team displayed was a 180-degree showing from that inaugural team. And with each game that followed, one notion crystalized: America no longer held the monopoly on the sport's talent; the world as a whole had caught up.

Could it have been an aberration? Perhaps. Could the young players have just been searching for their sea legs, unaware of the pitfalls and trap doors the Olympics could provide? Sure. After all, the 2004 games were the first summer Olympics to take place after the events of September 11, 2001, and there was a genuine fear emanating from the Americans that their safety was in danger as they entered Greece. Said Chris Sheridan of ESPN:

This was the first Olympics after 9/11. Everybody was hearing that the Greeks don't have their act together and it was going to be dangerous. There wasn't what you have now, a desire to play for the national team that was really overwhelming. There wasn't a program in which guys had come up through the select team or maybe through the U-16 or the U-18 team, which is what USA Basketball has now. It was more of a "Let's just pick the 12 best players we can and put them out there. Look we're Team USA; we are going to be able to beat everybody."

"I don't blame any of those kids [referring to Carmelo Anthony and LeBron James]," said team coach Larry Brown after the loss. "They followed the leadership of the older guys. They didn't handle the situation well; they were too worried about their playing time. They're all special players and they're having great years, but all the dribble-drive skills they possess don't matter against a zone, when the foreign teams have big guys who can just sit there, make you shoot a jump shot. And because we had the kids, we had no real point guard, no shooters, no role players.

"I got more calls from people—many of them not even involved with basketball, just coaches in other sports—saying that our success helped them because we were truly a team. And I think that's what we've gotten away from in our sport the last few years and maybe now we see what the Europeans are doing and we're starting to realize we have to do it differently."

But, as would play out over the following two weeks, the opening night saga against Puerto Rico was only a sign of things to come and can viewed through two very clear lenses.

One was the vast improvements from teams around the world. Everywhere Team USA turned, teams that once bowed at their feet now rolled out rosters full of NBA players, or of vastly improved talent that played together in a fluid, beautiful motion.

The second, clear as day to anyone watching, was the divisive, me-first personalities that ran rampant through the USA locker room.

* * *

Bob Whitsitt, who wore the moniker of "Trader Bob" during his tenure as the general manager of the Portland Trail Blazers, once quipped that he "wasn't a chemistry major" as he was piecing together a roster long on talent, but glued together with drug abusers, woman beaters, immature high schoolers, and moody malcontents who had worn out their welcome at previous stops.

The expression was quickly backed up; his Trail Blazers teams won a lot of games—including making back-to-back Western Conference finals appearances—but were better known for internal meltdowns, law-shattering antics away from the arena, and their epic meltdown in Game Seven of the 2000 Western Conference finals against the Los Angeles Lakers. Talent did in fact win; when it mattered most, however, chemistry was the one missing ingredient.

Whitsitt may as well have been forecasting Team USA. From the end of the 2004 NBA season, it was clear something was amiss as the roster building began in earnest that June. It seemed almost weekly that reports leaked from Team USA headquarters of players not investing in the process, or certain players loafing through, assured their spots were safe, or—and this was the one piece becoming more and more evident—feeling a disconnect from the top down, namely head coach Larry Brown.

Brown was coming off a miraculous year in which he took the Detroit Pistons to the NBA Finals, where they had upset the Los Angeles Lakers. Brown had struck gold with a perfectly ensembled cast of players that caught lightning in a bottle. He pushed all the right buttons with players such as Rip Hamilton, Ben Wallace, Rasheed Wallace, and Chauncey Billups. It was the perfect storm; after decades as a head coach, Brown had finally climbed to the top. But the experience countered the reputation he had built up over time. And that reputation—pedant and irascible—would come back and tear down the team as the games approached.

"I remember in the qualifier for the Olympics, Brown told Jason Kidd, 'Hey Jason, I know you're really good at the fast break, but I want you to stop at the free-throw line and throw a bounce pass to one of the wings,'" Richard Jefferson told NBC Olympics in 2017. "And you're sitting here talking to the second all-time leading assist guy and one of the most dominant point guards of all time. Truth be told, that's probably why nine guys decided that they didn't want to go do the Olympics."

Ah, yes, "The Ones That Got Away," as we'll call them. The list of players that backed out of Team USAs involvement in the Olympics could have, arguably, won Gold all by themselves. The reason for their absences were vast and speculative.

The blessed vows of matrimony kept players such as Vince Carter, Kevin Garnett, and Tracy McGrady away. Ray Allen—who's three-point ability would have been a clear difference-maker for the team filled with average to below-average shooters—was home with his pregnant fiancée. The aforementioned Kidd was not only at odds with Brown's coaching style but was also dealing with microfracture surgery that severely limited his play. Shaquille O'Neal, Jermaine O'Neal, and Ben Wallace were all coming off long playoff runs, and wanted to use the time for rest. Most notably, Kobe Bryant's trial for sexual assault was ongoing, making his involvement nearly impossible.

"Let's be serious. If we take Kobe and we take McGrady and we take, you know, Shaq—I mean, you gotta be kiddin' me," Daly told *GQ* in 2012. "I don't care how good they think their teams are. I really don't care."

The who's who of NBA stars watching on television depleted the team's talent to a point, but it was the clear lack of care that shone through. While guys like Iverson—who had battled a perilous reputation throughout his eight NBA seasons as a selfish, me-first player—were fully invested, too many players were there for their personal agendas, or simply lacked the understanding of what was at stake.

Where the 1992 team cast aside their monstrous egos for the betterment of the team, and used their skills in breathtaking teamwork, the 2004 squad played in a polar opposite manner.

"I don't use the word 'Dream Team,' okay? There was one Dream Team and only one Dream Team," said then commissioner David Stern. His words were the truest representation of the abomination that would play out.

With no clear leader—captains Iverson and Duncan were either ill-equipped to lead (Iverson) or averse to stepping up and taking charge (Duncan)—and as things went from bad, to worse, to *Holy shit, this is all crumbling*, too many holes opened up. The ship was sinking, and there was no one to keep it afloat.

Although he was unable to rally the squad during the tournament, Iverson—perhaps the least-likely player in 2004 to step up and take the full brunt of the blame, did just that, showcasing a humility that had been vacant prior.

"It's an honor to be named to this team," Iverson said in 2004 to Yahoo! Sports' Adrian Wojnarowski, who is now at ESPN. "It's something that you should cherish for the rest of your life. And honestly, this is something that I will cherish even without winning a gold medal. I feel like a special basketball player to make it to a team like this."

"He was never afraid to make himself front and center, even when the public unjustly wanted to make him the embodiment for the reasons they didn't like this team," Wojnarowski wrote shortly after the games. "And even rooted against it. ... He was willing to expose himself to the hits, the way no one else did here."

Outside of Iverson, excuses flowed from the mouths of the players after they finished the Games with a 5–3 record, including losses to Argentina, the eventual Gold medal winner, in the penultimate game. Heading into the Olympics, the idea that the USA was somehow about to be supplanted was beyond comprehension. Even years later, failure of recognition was rampant. "I think I'm being honest in saying that the NBA season is the priority for NBA players," said Grant Hill, which is code for *We got our asses handed to us, and we still cannot admit that reality.*

But that summer taught anyone who was paying attention that without their absolute best effort, the United States was no longer able to roll the ball out and win convincingly. The rest of the world had caught up.

The reign of terror was over.

* * *

Nathaniel Penn spoke with the most prominent folks who helped shape that summer of 2004 in his oral history story for *GQ*. From the players on the American roster, to players, reporters, coaches, and fans from other countries involved, Penn pieced together an entertaining and eye-opening tale of just how far America had dropped. What he discovered, though, was that the tournament was not lost though one game, or by one player, or strictly from better competition. What took Team USA down was a complete failure, from the top down, and from the arrogance and complacency that had built up over time.

Below is a small snippet of the piece, published with permission from Penn. The quotes, though small and quippy at times, tell a haunting tale of how American players, and the team as a whole, were looked at as the summer games approached:

Andrew Bogut *(center, Team Australia)*: "The Greek fans wanted U.S.A. to lose, because they're cocky, pound their chests. You see that in the NBA, but in Europe it's not respected."

"Pepe" Sanchez *(guard, Team Argentina)*: "A lot of great NBA players didn't come. Some of my teammates don't even know who the U.S. players are. I had to tell them, "Okay, this guy, he can shoot. That guy, he plays defense.""

Manu Ginóbili *(guard, Team Argentina)*: "The rest of the world is getting better. The U.S. is getting bored."

Deimante Staniuliene *(fan, Lithuania)*: "The Dream Team is dead. It's over. We play team basketball. You can't have an NBA attitude, not together. People have no root for the U.S.A. Because nobody likes what the U.S.A. is doing (to the) rest of the world."

Gregg Popovich *(assistant coach, Team USA)*: "You can't blame the U.S. players who came here. You can't blame them for wanting to sightsee and go to dinner. This isn't their end-all. This was a summer basketball trip."

Jorge Garbajosa *(forward, Team Spain)*: "Against us, they look worried. They didn't talk much when the game was close. But as soon as they ahead, they are chirping. Especially Richard Jefferson. What did he have? Six points?"

Šarūnas Jasikevicius *(guard, Team Lithuania)*: "The worst talker on the court was Shawn Marion. He kept saying "miss" when I would shoot. And I kept making them. The ball was coming off my fingers, and he said, "Miss, you fuck. Miss. You're in the NBA now. Miss like you should, fuck." After a while, he stopped, because I kept making them."

Mario Pesquera *(coach, Team Spain)*: "I'm tired of the opinions, the articles, that say the U.S. team is the best. The Spanish team demonstrated that they were the best team, because we just lost one game. No other team did that. "

Ginóbili: "I saw their roster and I knew we would beat them."

Popovich: "Against Argentina, Tim was officiated like he's never going to be officiated in the NBA. There were times he was absolutely knocked to the floor, kicked over, and trampled—and no call?"

Bogut: "The body language of some players on the bench was terrible. I think they were getting frustrated with not getting playing time. There were guys not even paying attention during the time-outs."

Sanchez: "They didn't shake our hands after the game. They walk away. We don't care. That's them. "

Alexander Avramovski *(fan, Macedonia)*: "Before the Olympics, we were watching the U.S. play Serbia. We got excited, because the U.S. team is not connected with each other."

Fabricio Oberto *(center, Team Argentina)*: "We were inside the stadium, waiting to go out to get the medals. We were singing songs, like soccer fans. The Americans were very quiet. It was like two faces—twelve players on one side, singing, and the other guys very quiet, looking at us. "

Massimo Bulleri *(guard, Team Italy)*: "It was really strange to see American players below us on the podium. When we played against them in Germany, a few days before the Olympics, I stepped onto the floor and said to myself, "I am only dreaming. I am playing against my idols."

The excuses flowed from the mouths of the American players and coaches. The eye rolls careened off the faces of everyone else. The message as the 2004–05 NBA season began was that the United States had embarrassed themselves, sleepwalking, in-fighting, and dicking around just enough to get taken down.

For Team USA, retribution would come four years later, in 2008, when the "Redeem Team," led by Bryant, James, Anthony, and newcomers such as Chris Paul, Dwight Howard, and Chris Bosh took home gold in Beijing, China. Internally, for the NBA and Team USA, order had been restored. For them, the gold had returned to its rightful owner; the arrogance and cocky swagger had returned, too.

Outside of the United States, though—and as would be solidified for years to come—a different narrative had already been created. Because while folks in the 50 states had viewed 2004 as a blip in the radar, around the world, another angle was created—one that would prove to be truer than any fabrication the United States could make up.

Basketball around the globe had caught up to America . . . and the players responsible were on their way.

Chapter Eleven

INVESTING OVERSEAS

Team USA's loss at the 2004 Olympics may have knocked fans in the United States over. Many of whom, for all of the reasons one would expect, assumed the national team would roll into Greece and walk out with the gold, just as they had the three previous Olympics.

That's what the everyman thought. For those in the know, however, Argentina's victory was not surprising in the least. As the game of basketball has continued its steady rise in popularity stateside, the byproduct of that has been felt everywhere.

"The game has become more popular in Europe," J. R. Holden, a two-time EuroLeague champion for CSKA Moscow who now scouts overseas for the Detroit Pistons, told CBS Sports in 2016. "You had speckles of players. Sabonis. Kukoč. But you didn't have seven guys on a team that could play in the NBA. Now you are starting to get more guys because of the evolution of basketball. Now you see kids who aren't just wearing soccer jerseys, but more basketball jerseys."

As the number of international players suiting up in the NBA has grown, so, too, have the eyeballs from other parts of the world. No longer are small pockets of space occupying the best players outside of the United States;

"Ten, fifteen years ago, you could go to three and four countries—Croatia, Serbia, Lithuania, Argentina—and get 90 percent of your work done. But you can't do that anymore. If it's a 14-day trip, I'm probably going to hit 12 countries," Pete Philo, the Indiana Pacers' director of international scouting, who also worked for the Dallas Mavericks and Minnesota Timberwolves, told HoopsHype in 2015. "And let me tell you something: You get tired, and you need a couple of days to recoup. The demanding travel is the most challenging thing about being an international scout."

Perhaps no one on the planet is more versed than Philo in not only the role international players have played in reshaping the way the NBA is played, but also about what it takes for them to arrive: the routes NBA scouts have to take to mine for the diamonds in the rough, the hoops some players still have to jump through to make it over, and the challenges and obstacles they face after they arrive in a foreign land.

Philo co-founded EuroCamp in 2003, told *Bleacher Report* in 2014 that the camp was designed to create an "exposure camp for some of the younger international kids" while also giving NBA personnel an up-close view on players that might had previously gone unnoticed.

"It's the next big thing," Philo continued. "A lot of people from the NBA were there. Even agents were really excited about it because they learned how to save time on recruiting talent, and head coaches and assistant coaches in college learned how to evaluate better. We shared philosophies, some evaluation formulas. We taught people how to really look at things, and what translates and what doesn't from overseas to the NBA."

Philo, who was mentored by Donnie Nelson—the man responsible for the drafting of Šarūnas Marčiulionis—has now taken a special interest in helping up-and-coming scouts take their leap into the big time.

Marčiulionis—who was drafted in 1987 and made his debut in 1989, becoming the first Soviet to play in the NBA—was once described as being able to "jump like David Thompson, shoot like Larry Bird or pass like Magic Johnson." His impact on the game is sometimes lost in the shuffle, but to those close to the sport state that his game speaks for itself. Because of these facts, Marčiulionis was inducted into the Naismith Memorial Basketball Hall of Fame in 2014.

"There really are no words to describe Sarunas' worthiness in the Hall of Fame," Tommy Sheppard, the Washington Wizards' senior vice president of basketball operations, told Bruce Jenkins of *Sports Illustrated.* "This is a man who always had a heartbeat for his country, who made people realize they didn't have to stand there and take what was forced upon them. His whole life was about freedom, and giving back. It's straight out of Hollywood casting."

"The way he lived was all about heart and determination, someone who wouldn't take no for an answer," said longtime friend Donnie Nelson, a key figure in Marciulionis's life. "And that's exactly how he played the game."

As Peter de Jonge wrote about Marčiulionis in the *New York Times Magazine*:

Now he has somehow slain the dragon of Sovintersport and made it to the N.B.A. And even if he can't keep every cent of his $1.3 million a year contract, he can certainly afford anything he has ever wanted. But it is his nature to be wary. Asked if he would go out of his way to form friendships with his new teammates, he replies: "I believe friendship is born in moments of victory and defeat. They are not made."

As Pete Philo mentioned to *Bleacher Report* in 2014, so much of the scouting game is, quite simply, building relationships necessary to be successful.

"People tell me they want to be an international scout and I'm like, 'Who do you know overseas?' It's not about evaluating talent. To me, that's secondary now. It's relationships, it's getting contract information, it's being able to get into a practice where they shut Americans out, especially NBA personnel. You've got to know people you trust and how to navigate overseas. I've been very lucky because I ran the EuroCamp for nine years, from 2003 to '11. A lot of people had to come through me to get their players in, so I built a lot of relationships, and that's helped me to this day because now I can get information—contract, medical and background studies—pretty quickly."

The other annual event that has helped bring exposure, at a very limited cost to NBA teams, is the NBA Summer League. The league hosts two separate events—the first in Salt Lake City, Utah, and the main event in Las Vegas, Nevada.

For players, executives, and fans—who can watch the games for a quarter of the price of a regular NBA game, in smaller venues that are littered with vacationing NBA stars—summer league is essentially a two-week look into what the future of the league may look like.

"Everyone is here," Simone Casali, GM of Olimpia Milano in Italy, told *Grantland* in 2015. Milano has won 28 Serie A titles, multiple domestic cup wins, and three EuroLeague titles; they're also the former home of current Houston Rockets head coach Mike D'Antoni, as well as NBA veteran Danilo Gallinari. "It's a mess because it's a bunch of information. And it's a bunch of people. Everybody wants to talk, understand, know. You can have a different point of view because you can talk to journalists, agents, that maybe don't know your league that well. It's a web. You start from one point and it grows."

But, as Casali points out, it's also a chance to see players hoping to enter the NBA—either by way of college, from overseas, or even the G-League, the NBA's developmental league.

"Summer League is the place to find different levels of players, playing together," he said. "You have to balance the level of the competition going on. Who is playing, who they are playing with, who they are playing against? Then it's not the truth, because the defense in the summer league is [not as good as] in our league. But you know that everybody is trying to play his best because they're looking for a contract."

After the opening year of the EuroCamp in 2003, then Argentina's Olympic win the following year, the role of international scouts skyrocketed among NBA teams. While Argentina's gold medal team featured five players who were already in the NBA, many of the other teams in that year's event squared up against the USA with players largely unknown to the best league in the world. That alone was enough to pique the interest of owners who wondered if the next Ginóbili, or Petrović, or Kukoč was tearing up leagues outside of their scope.

Thus, the "International Boom" was in full tilt.

* * *

He wasn't always known as the "Czar of the Telestrator."

Long before Mike Fratello teamed with Marv Albert as an announcer, calling the action of the best players in the world, he was busy leading them. And in 1988, his Atlanta Hawks squad traveled all the way to Russia—on owner Ted Turner's dime—as part of a two-week exhibition tournament where they would square off against the Soviet national team, becoming the first NBA team to play in the USSR. Fratello describes the event as a "breakthrough type of situation," and his hindsight is hard to argue with. It had been just three years since Stern's infamous "America's Game" jab when the Blazers had drafted Sabonis (not so coincidentally from the same part of the world, no doubt), and thanks in large part to the cold war tensions thawing, the Hawks were on a sort of good-will mission.

While it would have, at the time, been hard to predict the impact the trip would have on the future of basketball—"I look back on it fondly now, but at the time, what we did for two weeks was we basically ate cucumbers, tomatoes and warm vodka," longtime Hawks radio voice Steve Holman told *Sports Illustrated* in 2017. But more than thirty years later, the impact is undeniable. At the time, the unspoken truth was that Turner was eyeing his upcoming Goodwill Games, and the Soviet's involvement and the NBA was seeing the potential in international inclusion as the driving forces behind the trip. But what came from it was far greater than any side could have predicted.

"The league approved this because it was really the beginning of David Stern looking at the globality of the NBA. One of the first steps had to be players from Eastern Europe," says Kim Bohuny, who helped run the trip for TBS and is now the NBA's vice president of international basketball operations. Bohuny had been in charge of research and athlete profiles at the Goodwill Games and was already familiar with the Soviet players. "There were so many great players behind the Eastern European wall, and part of this was to bring it down for the NBA."

The USSR had taken many trips over the previous years to play colleges in the United States, but by the Hawks and NBA stepping foot in their motherland, the hand was extended from Stern, essentially opening the floodgates for international players to arrive in the USA.

Now, thanks to Fratello, Turner, Stern, and a host of other forward-thinking people—even if, like in Stern's case, it took them a long time—the views of international players' abilities to compete in the NBA have almost flipped.

"It's heading that direction," said Philo. "At the end of the day, five things matter in terms of productivity and playing in the NBA: speed, skill, size, athleticism, and feel. If you have those five things, you're usually a really good NBA player, a starter, or an All-Star. From there, it goes into your rotation player, and that can be more skill specific, position specific. It wouldn't surprise me, because people are playing the game at a high level everywhere."

What was lost for so long, as scouts and owners focused more on the levels of competition as the determining factor of whether a player's skills would translate, was that, at the end of the day, basketball is a game played the same across all platforms. Dribble, shoot, pass.

"They get footwork at a very, very young age," Philo told CBS Sports in 2016 "They get taught how to run pick and rolls. They get drilled on spacing. They get drilled on ball movement. When they catch the ball, they have rules. You either drive it immediately, you shoot it immediately, or you pass it immediately. You do not hold it. Those are foreign rules. Those are the important things to them. They don't have ESPN or the networks that promote flashy play or dunks or whatnot. Where in our country, that's exciting for us. Over there, they don't have that. They don't turn to that. They play a certain style, and they play it well."

All it took was a few transformational players, a world tour, an Argentinian Olympics medal, and a host of new-age difference-makers for the light bulbs to fully go off.

"You don't see Ben Simmons coming over here [from Australia] and saying, 'I don't understand what the coach is saying,'" J. R. Holden, a two-time EuroLeague champion for CSKA Moscow who now scouts overseas for the Detroit Pistons, told CBS Sports in 2016. "You think of Tony Parker, he had to learn English and all the terminology to play at the level he's playing at."

There are still vast obstacles a scout must face when trying to find the next superstar to bring back to the states, just as there are for any college coach trying to find the next high school blue-chipper. The biggest obstacle is perhaps the lifestyle the scouts have to face. The travel is extensive and can be abrupt.

"This is a very nomadic business," said Philo to Michael Creppy of *The Undefeated*. "You have to be prepared to pack up and move at any time. It can be for a variety of reasons: for a better contract or, a team's financial issues, whatever. Lastly, after the first few months in a country, it begins to be a grind on the court. Personally, I think America is paradise and I could not live in another country permanently. Over the course of a season, which usually lasts seven to eight months, basketball is the easy part. The hard part is after those two to four hours of practice or games, you have the rest of the day to get away from your friends and family. I've missed countless Thanksgivings, birthdays, and family events. I tell players all the time, if you don't play basketball, playing overseas will be difficult, and no amount of money will give you peace."

The other obstacle—the one that kept NBA teams away for so long—still lingers in the back of scouts' minds. For them, there is no greater fear than returning home, championing for a player, watching their team draft that player, then realizing, almost instantaneously, that they're not cut out for the competition.

"Over here, college players are playing against maybe the oldest is 23—a fifth-year senior, transfer. Over there, guys they're going against could be 35, 28. How do you measure that? The experience, the physicality. That is still the hardest part of the job, trying to figure out what's going to transition. Mistakes are made when you automatically think because someone's a good player, he should be a good player in the NBA. But it doesn't work like that. Everything is different overseas—rules, rotations, terminology, size, length."

* * *

For every player that has arrived as an unknown and morphed into a star, there are far more who's time never came. Perhaps no player best exemplifies that than Darko Miličić.

In 2003, the NBA was abuzz with an Akron high schooler who would be the first pick in the draft: LeBron James. His hometown team, the Cleveland Cavaliers, saw the ping pong balls bounce their way, landing the No. 1 pick.

Aside from James, future Hall-of-Famers Carmelo Anthony (3rd pick), Chris Bosh (4th), and Dwyane Wade (5th) came calling. Of the 58 players drafted, 28 would play at least six seasons. It is arguably the best draft in league history, highlighted by the heavyweights at the top.

After those names, the next thought almost always goes to the second pick in the draft. Miličić was a tantalizing prospect, prompting the Detroit Pistons to take a chance on the 7-footer from Serbia.

Mostly watching from the bench, Miličić played 11 seasons with six different teams before retiring from the league after the 2012–13 season with a career average of just 6 points per game. The Pistons would win the NBA title in 2004; Miličić averaged 1.4 points in 4.7 minutes per game. Anthony would average 21.0 points and 6.1 rebounds with the Nuggets in his rookie campaign, kickstarting a career that is still flourishing in 2020.

Miličić is far from alone; since 2002, 10 international players have been drafted in the top 20 of their respective drafts, only to make little to no impact in the league. On such flop arrived in 2007: China's Yi Jianlian, drafted 6th by the Bucks. Another 7-footer, Yi came to the USA with his own mythical fables; most notably his nickname "The Chairman," given after rumors persisted in the summer of 2007 that, in attempts to impress NBA scouts ahead of the upcoming draft, put on a splendid and detailed workout… against a folding chair. Although no videos of the encounter can be found on the internet, Chris Mannix wrote for *The Vertical* in 2017 that, yes, the legend is real. Sitting in on Yi's workout with the Sacramento Kings, he shares the often-wondered story:

> First, there were a lot of drills that showcased Yi's athleticism. At 7-feet, 246 pounds, Yi was an excellent athlete, and I recall seeing a lot of him getting out in transition. Second, he wasn't working out against anybody. Not unusual—it makes little sense putting a raw, Chinese player in against a more polished college star.
>
> And third: There was a chair. I don't recall Yi posting up against it (that wouldn't make much sense, anyway) or dribbling around it. But I remember when Yi was running through catch-and-shoot drills, the chair was used as a prop for a screener. He would run around the chair, catch and fire midrange jumpers.

The lore of Yi to this day is more interesting than his actual career; Yi would play just five seasons in the league, averaging 7.9 points per game.

Through it all, though—the challenges, opportunities, hits and misses—the biggest change is the one that appears to be here for good. The NBA, after years of ignoring the possibilities right in front of them, are no longer shying away from the rest of the world, and the talent that is waiting to be plucked.

Chapter Twelve

REHABBING IMAGES

The shrinking of the basketball community around the globe has myriad benefits; one that gets lost in the shuffle is the liberation players can feel in extending their careers overseas once their time in the NBA has come to an end. Some players—such as Josh Childress, the former Stanford Cardinal standout who abruptly left the NBA in 2008 to go play for Olympiacos Piraeus in Greece—came as a blindside of sorts, a player in his prime seeking greener pastures. Others, such T. J. Ford, used their second chance in Europe to bounce back from debilitating injuries that robbed his once promising careers.

And in more dire instances, leaving one's motherland can be a literal rehabilitation.

Case in point, former NBA center Robert Swift.

Swift was selected as the 12th overall pick of the 2004 NBA Draft by the (then) Seattle SuperSonics, after an illustrious career for Garces Memorial High School in Bakersfield, California, and then later as the centerpiece of the Bakersfield High School team.

Swift entered the draft at a crucial time for big men; Shaquille O'Neal was beginning to tail off and Yao Ming had yet to fully find his footing in the league. The role of the traditional NBA center—that of the lumbering, methodical, back-to-the-basket behemoth—was nearing the end of its dominant run.

For Swift, the timing was perfect. From the outside looking in, he possessed none of those discerning traits. Swift was 7-foot-1 and 245 pounds, lucidly pale, with a tuft of red hair—but, when he was on the court, he was a small forward trapped in a much larger man's body.

His footwork was lightning quick. His touch around the basket was undeniable. His instincts on defense were beyond his years. As a senior, playing in the McDonald's All-American game, Swift—one of seven players who would jump straight to the NBA from high school in that year's draft—was a showstopper. Despite the presence of future NBA All-Stars such as Dwight Howard, LaMarcus Aldridge, and Rajon Rondo (among others), Swift never once seemed out of place.

So when the SuperSonics drafted Swift, they envisioned him as the dawning of a new era. Gone were Shawn Kemp and Gary Payton and Sam Perkins. Their best player, Ray Allen, was twenty-nine and not one designed to carry a franchise by himself. With Swift, the franchise could market the youngster as the next phase for the franchise, which had been strangled by rumors of their displacement.

With the memories fresh from his high school days, and the dominant performance at the All-American game, Swift arrived at training camp ready to embrace his role.

There was one slight issue, which became apparent early.

He couldn't shoot.

Couldn't dribble.

Couldn't pass.

In high school, Swift was between 8 to 10 inches taller than almost every player he went up against, showcasing him as a dominant, game-changing defender.

The All-American game, in hindsight, was a glorified flag-basketball game, with very little resistance. Even the most gangly, awkward players were allowed to shine.

But to truly understand Swift's struggles, you have to go back. Back before the falling out in Seattle and Oklahoma City. Back before the drugs and alcohol and bullet wounds that punctured his existence. You have to go back to 2003, to the streets of Bakersfield. To poverty and pressure. Because for Swift, a millionaire overnight in the Emerald City, this is where his story's arc turned. It's where, just one year before their son struck it rich, the Swift parents signed on the dotted line for their fifth bankruptcy.

Swift's mother, Rhonda, had battled through multiple rounds of cancer and surgeries by the time he had entered the draft. The eighteen-year-old was just two years into being able to drive and, through no fault of his own, completely in charge of saving his family from financial ruin.

What Swift needed was a support system designed to nurture the young man. At the time, the handfuls of players who had jumped straight from high school to the pros had, mostly, found success. Kobe Bryant was already on a Hall of Fame track. So, too, was Kevin Garnett. But unlike Swift, the Bryants and Garnetts came prepackaged. They either looked the part (Garnett), or came from backgrounds that bred them for the spotlight (Bryant).

Swift was eighteen, on his own, rich, with a shackled family back home and, thanks to his deficiencies, designated to the end of the bench. Any clear role he would have with the franchise appeared to be years in the future. And he had no one. No player development coach attached to his massive hips, guiding him through the tribulations that followed; no support system eager to engage and make him a better player. Nothing. He was adrift in a gray, drizzly city. His pockets were lined, but nothing else about the situation set him up for success.

From the moment he was drafted, the organization—from the coach on down—treated Swift like a hulking misfit. Established players viewed the teenager as a drag-along rather than a cog in the wheel. In Swift they saw a project, not a prodigy.

The SuperSonics we're coming off a dismal 2003–04 season, where they finished 37–45, good for fifth place in the Pacific Division. Nate McMillan, "Mr. Sonic," as he had been crowned from his playing days with the team, was entering his fourth full season as the franchise's coach (he coached them for 67 games in 2000–01 after the team had fired Paul Westphal). The SuperSonics had been treading water for the better part of the decade since their mystical NBA Finals run in 1996. They were never truly bad, but never truly good, either. Aside from their 61-win campaign in 1998, where they were bounced in the second round in five games by the Los Angeles Lakers, things in the Emerald City had been . . . irrelevant. Ken Griffey Jr., Alex Rodriguez, Edgar Martínez—those names had come and gone from the Seattle Mariners, the city's Major League Baseball team.

The Sonics were still two years from landing the No. 2 overall pick, which would reveal itself to be a player by the name of Kevin Durant.

So, no—in 2004, what the SuperSonics needed was a jolt. Electricity. High-flying, fast-breaking, rim-rattling, three-point marksman energy.

So, when then commissioner David Stern announced Robert Swift as the newest addition to the franchise, it wasn't just the collective fan base letting out their audible groans. It was his future teammates and some coaches, too.

As Chris Ballard wrote for *Sports Illustrated* in 2016:

But then David Stern is at the podium announcing the 12th selection, and Swift hears his name. A lottery pick? Moments later, the Sonics head coach calls. Says Nate McMillan: "I'm looking forward to actually seeing you play." Three weeks later Swift became a millionaire. Now, neither he nor his wife will work for the foreseeable future. Alex's college tuition will be covered. They've made it. All of them.

Napoleon Dynamite. That's what the Sonics players call him. The kid is big but not ready. Not emotionally, not physically. He never talks in practice or team meetings. "You had to pry two words out of him," recalls Dwight Daub, the Seattle strength coach.

Five seasons (missing 2006–07 to a knee injury) and 97 games later (with just 34 starts), Swift was on his own, out of the league. He was twenty-three, with no education and no future in the only thing he had ever loved.

In 2013, his once pristine home no longer existed. When the front door cracked open, the first rays of sunlight entered, the cocktail of moldy cigarette butts, burnt to their last drag, mixed with dog feces. The smell bounced in unison with the state of the home, the inside better resembling a gutted-out home dressed up as a haunted house. Scattered inside, among other glints of happiness—recruitment letters from colleges, a picture of a vibrant Swift next to Yao Ming—were memories of a once-promising career washed away.

Then there were the bullet holes in the basement. The guns—dozens of them—in all shapes and sizes. Crusted-out pizza boxes. An anarchy symbol drawn out in blue painter's tape. Five half-empty bottles of booze. Perhaps most symbolic, a broken-down Conestoga wagon, a covered wagon used extensively during the late eighteenth century and the nineteenth century. Broken down and washed up, it seemed, much like its former owner.

Swift had recently vacated the property; the latest eviction warning was the one he finally heeded. When the new owners of the property arrived, the aforementioned mess and stench had met them head on.

Nothing about it said an NBA player had been the cause of the disaster, but that was the reality.

The house, the past, was a sinister reminder of fame gone wrong; of family and financial pressure caving in and destroying a young soul.

But outside of the house, outside of the state, and outside of the country, a new beginning had sprung. Two years prior, he had gotten a new agent, who had begun working to clear him for a passport. Overseas teams had been reaching out. He just needed to be, as he says, "passport ready." So, Swift went to the passport agency, applied, and then waited and hoped.

It worked. The passport, and new life, were approved. Tokyo Apache, a professional team in Japan coached by Bob Hill—who had coached Swift his final few years in Seattle—wanted him, and Swift accepted. The rehabilitation was under way.

Swift would still battle his demons—in October 2014, police raided the house of Trygve Bjorkstam, who was an alleged heroin and methamphetamine dealer, who had a collection of eighteen guns. Inside, they found Swift living in the home, and in possession of a sawed-off shotgun. In November 2014, police charged Swift with unlawful possession of a short-barreled shotgun. Later, on January 8, 2015, Swift was arrested by police for involvement in an armed home invasion attempt, where he claimed he was high on drugs at the time of the incident.

Since then, he's been back overseas. In 2018, he signed with Círculo Gijón in Spain, where he has been, primarily, since. Now, Swift is living in a four-bedroom apartment with Círculo Gijón's three other American players. His time playing professionally away from the NBA—from the temptations and bad people he associated himself with—were the most successful in his life, both on and off the court.

But not all the stories are ones of despair. While there are indeed times where the pay is thin and the accommodations sparing, there is much opportunity for success. Just take a look at Justin Doellman, who went undrafted after graduating from Xavier in 2007 and has had decade-plus career overseas, including stops in Italy, Turkey, Germany, Russia, and Montenegro.

"It is kind of funny," Doellman said to David Driver for his "All Over the Map" article, published in *Xavier Nation* magazine. "A lot of [people] think it is more of a semi-pro league and wonder *when are you going to find a real job?* You're making great money and people have no idea. It's not public knowledge."

My first contract was just under six figures coming right out of college. . . . NBA guys can make $400,000 or $500,000 a year over there [overseas]. If you do it correctly you can set yourself up and retire at age thirty-five. My close circle knows that is my main source of income. They all kind of understand we have chosen this and we have done pretty well overseas."

* * *

Josh Akognon, who played professionally in China, Spain, and Serbia—and who also played in three games for the Dallas Mavericks during the 2012–13 season—spoke to EuroHoops. net in 2019 on the difference in game play overseas, specifically between China and the NBA:

You get a lot of shots in the CBA [China Basketball Association]. They really don't care too much about your defense. Towards the end of the game, they want to see you play some defense against the other Americans. The main thing in China is to try and get your points up, and to win. How you get to scoring or winning, is not as important as it is in Europe, where everything is so structured and everyone looks at every single shot, as kind of a big thing. The NBA is a numbers game. Europe is the strictest of all three and it's the toughest to play in.

"The NBA, you have the best players in the world. The greatest competition in the world. Nothing can ever compete with the NBA. Guys are playing at the highest level and you can't beat that," Dorell Wright, who played in the NBA for 11 seasons before retiring in 2015, told EuroHoops.net. He spent one season, 2017–18, playing for Brose Bamberg in Germany. "EuroLeague, it's the second-best competition in the world. You are playing against all the international competition at a young age [before they get to the NBA]. The international game is evolving. Young players are getting the opportunity to play at the second-highest level at a very young age, like Luka Dončić. Some of the best American players are also coming to Europe to play in the EuroLeague.

"The EuroLeague is great because it is more orientated to the team. There's almost never going to be a player scoring 20+ points every game. It's going to be a group of guys scoring 8–12 points. That's impressive. Averaging 12–14 points in Europe is like averaging 22 in the NBA. A lot of people don't understand that when international prospects from Europe get drafted in the NBA and they average just six points per game. It's so hard to score in Europe. It's different. You have to grind it out in Europe to score, while the NBA is more showtime. The atmosphere is something crazy."

Wright is becoming more of the rule than the exception; a player who carved out a nice, long career in the NBA before playing overseas. The money, and the fame, are hard for a player in his mid-thirties to turn down. But one player stands above them all: Stephon Marbury. After a wild tenure in the NBA, he left for China to become, arguably, the most popular player in China (not including Yao, of course). He played eight seasons in the Chinese Basketball Association, winning three titles with the Beijing Ducks. Marbury's rehabilitation wasn't like Swift's, where drugs and alcohol had taken grip of his career, but the cleansing of his experience in China was just as dramatic. He was viewed most often as a malcontent during his time in the NBA; in China, he was a folk hero (and a statue, located outside the Beijing Ducks' arena.

As he embraced the crowd on the night of his retirement, with the home crowd chanting his name, Marbury took the microphone, his parting words perhaps best describing the experiences so many American-born players are finding in leagues around the world.

"Ending my basketball career here in China completes me. This is it—no NBA, no anywhere. This is the way it's supposed to end, here with you and only you."

Over the past decade, a plethora of NBA players have found resurgence in China and, because of that, the Chinese Basketball Association has resuscitated more careers than can be imagined. Tyler Hansbrough, who in his four years at the University of North Carolina became one of the more immortal and polarizing players college basketball has seen, never found his footing in the NBA. Although he lasted seven seasons with the Indiana Pacers, Toronto Raptors, and Chicago Bulls, "Psycho T," as he was known in college for his maniacal style of play, never found a niche. His career averages of 6.7 points and 4.2 rebounds were modest at best. But his time in China has been more in-line with his college days; during his first three seasons, he has averaged 23 points and 11 rebounds.

Hansbrough is in one of a handful of recent NBA players who have found refuge in China. Jimmer Fredette, Greg Oden, Steve Francis, Metta World Peace, Gilbert Arenas, and others have shone bright in the world's second most famous basketball league.

Chapter Thirteen

GROWING THE BRAND

As the 2018–19 NBA regular season tipped off—the year in which the Greek-born Giannis Antetokounmpo would win the MVP, and the league's lone international franchise—the Toronto Raptors—would win the title, there were a total of 108 international players in the league. The Raptors led the way with the most foreign-born players on the roster for a fifth consecutive year.

"I think symbolically," NBA commissioner Adam Silver said after the Raptors had secured their first-ever title, "having our first finals outside the United States maybe has a big impact on countries that follow the NBA but don't have teams, whether that be in Asia or whether that be in Latin America. I think as we look back in time at the NBA calendar, I mean, this clearly is a marker of sorts."

The headliner of the NBA Finals—and, really, the entire season—had been Kawhi Leonard, the former San Antonio Spurs star who had found his way to Toronto as perhaps the best one-year-rental any team had ever found. However, it was the supporting cast, which included players from all over the globe—Lithuania, Spain, Republic of the Congo, the United Kingdom, Cameroon, and Saint Lucia.

And it was Pascal Siakam—a player who had struggled to find any solid ground in the NBA during his first two seasons—that may find his name among the most impactful players when history looks back at the Raptors' championship run. The Cameroon-born star, who began to make waves for the Raptors early the 2018 season, has since blossomed into a full-blown star.

And, much like his fellow countryman Joel Embiid, he's directly linked to the roads being paved for African players looking for their opportunity.

"I think that a lot of kids don't think that this is possible so just me being able to be here today and telling them 'hey, look at me, I was a scrawny little kid from Cameroon who couldn't think about this moment,' but here I am as a champion," Siakam said.

As the final seconds ticked off the clock on June 13 inside Oracle Arena in Oakland, California, with his first NBA title wrapped up, draped over Siakim's shoulders, was the Cameroon flag. "I just want to tell them that it is possible and if you believe in something you need to go out there and work hard for it. It might sound cliché, but it's the truth, and I'm the proof."

The Raptors' victory didn't usher in a new era for the league; that had been done years prior, when individual stars entered and made lasting impacts. What it did was insert the final pin of validation for a league that was truly beginning to understand the value of an expansive perspective: that a roster made predominantly of international players could not just carry their own weight, but eclipse the highest mountain, disemboweling one of the great dynasties in the process.

Not only did the Raptors defeat the Golden State Warriors, led by future Hall of Famers Kevin Durant, Stephen Curry, and Klay Thompson—beating them four games to two—but they did so with relative ease.

And they did it with flair.

"It meant a lot having guys on this team from different countries and speaking different languages . . . it brought us close together," Siakam told the *Sentinel* newspapers after the title parade in the summer of 2019. "With different languages and cultures, I think it represents Toronto, in general, having that diversity."

In the aftermath of the Raptors' victory, when the parades ended and the last of the champagne droplets had dried, the NBA did what it always did—it kept rolling.

The draft came and went. Free agents flirted across the country, assimilating in various regions. The talk of the Raptors' demise—Kawhi Leonard would relocate to Hollywood and the Los Angeles Clippers—made barely a blip on any talk show. Unsurprisingly, the franchise's title run was viewed with a side-eye, a cute story until the real show could begin. The summer of 2019 would be dominated by LeBron James and Anthony Davis teaming up for the Los Angeles Lakers, coaching carousels, the dysfunction of the Philadelphia 76ers, and myriad other subplots. But for the future growth and development of the league, the Raptors' championship carried much larger, long-term ramifications. It showcased the character and basketball spirit of a city known more for hockey (and baseball). It highlighted, to the highest level, the way players from multiple backgrounds can come together and play a brand of basketball outlandish enough to take down one of the most dominant runs the NBA had seen.

For the Raptors' first-year head coach Nick Nurse, it was the crowning moment for yet another outsider, a man seen as perhaps the least likely coach to stand atop the mountain.

"[Nurse] exudes a lot of confidence in our team," assistant coach Adrian Griffin told CBS Sports in 2019. "And I think our team has taken over his personality, that we're expected to win, we're expected to play well, we're expected to play harder than our opponent and we're never out of a game."

Raptors president Masai Ujiri is the perfect embodiment of the franchise, and of the new wave of the NBA in general. There's no nepotism in his success; no clear path to stardom cut from his white skin and Ivy league education. He's Nigerian; born in Bournemouth, a coastal town on the south coast of England. He first attended Bismarck State Community College before graduating at Montana State.

Coming from behind, when no one else thought it could be done? Sounds a lot like the city he brought a title.

"I said it when I came here: I know this city will win," Ujiri said before the Finals started. "It's not me or anybody. There's something about it here and sports. It comes around."

* * *

Before March 11, 2020, when Covid-19 brought the entire sports world to a halt, the NBA had been making tremendous inroads across the globe—not only in their own product, but in expanding the overall NBA brand.

Back in 2011, the league hosted their first-ever regular season game in London; the game itself was a dud, but the impact was made. When the (then) New Jersey Nets took down the Toronto Raptors, 116–103, the debut had come and gone, leaving fans and media alike draped in their seats, eyes half-open, flat soda the only thing keeping them awake. But the bigger picture was there: much like the NFL had been doing, the NBA, too, was setting foot in foreign soil.

"To be honest I didn't think it would work to bring it here," Ryan Brazier, 21, said before the game as the teams' mascots pranced, twisted and flipped their way onto the court while tossing soft, branded souvenirs into the crowd. "But it's pretty busy even though it's all so American."

The next steps taken after the (somewhat) successful London debut were the possibilities of expanding not just the actual NBA product, but the possibility of creating new leagues in various continents.

Thus, the idea for the Basketball Africa League, a new collaboration between the NBA and the sport's global governing body FIBA, was announced in February 2019.

"This league will be fully operated by the NBA," Amadou Gallo Fall, the NBA's vice president for Africa, told Reuters by phone from Johannesburg. "Our expertise and best practices will be on display."

"It's a big celebration. It is a dream come true for all of us," Dikembe Mutombo, a Democratic Republic of the Congo native and Basketball Hall of Famer, told *The Undefeated*. "I was fortunate enough to play this game and dreamed of something like this happening in the continent. Today, we see that. I don't have to explain the importance of it to myself."

"We did this because players like Dikembe pointed to the opportunity that existed, not just in basketball, but the sports industry throughout the continent," said NBA commissioner Adam Silver. "He and I have been there together at least four times since I've been commissioner. And through conversations with FIBA and local ministers of sport, we realize that there is enormous opportunity to continue to grow the game. There are a lot of young players in Africa who know about the success of Mutombo, but don't understand how to pursue those opportunities. Dikembe was very fortunate to come to school in the

United States and be at Georgetown and have the benefit of fantastic coaching and mentoring. Of course, many players in Africa would not know who to turn to. We know that by building this basketball infrastructure, it's going to create generations of new Dikembe Mutombos. On top of that, it can become an economic engine for all of Africa."

What the league can do—not only for the NBA, but for the local African spirit—is not lost. The division across the continent has been prevalent for decades, and for some, they view the new league as a way for people all over Africa to rally around a common goal.

"In the close future, we will be able to talk about a united Africa as well," Bismack Biyombo, a native of the Democratic Republic of the Congo, told Marc Spears in 2017. "Africa has always been a divided country where everybody wants to do their own thing. The next generation is now understanding how to work together. And then they need help growing the economy of Africa because now we are going to have diverse things growing around this game and BWB. This is important. This is something I wished I had growing up. The only way kids leave the country is to go abroad, not to go to another African country. Now, they see what is in other African countries and see what the other countries are facing. It's a game changer."

The economic impact could be huge as well.

"It's going to create more jobs," said Ujiri. "It's going to create more opportunity for people. If you look at the NBA and how many jobs it creates and revenue and how it brings people together, we need that on the continent."

And for guys like Embiid, Biyombo, and a new generation of young players who have traveled from Africa to the United States, it's a chance to be a part of their own door-opening mission.

"Everybody knows who Dikembe Mutombo, Hakeem Olajuwon and Luol Deng is," Gallo Fall told *The Undefeated*. "We have a great plan in the NBA that is attentive and young people have an infinity to because of the intersections with music, fashion and the whole lifestyle."

* * *

The NBA has a long and proud history with players from Africa. The most famous is Hakeem Olajuwon, who was drafted by the Houston Rockets in 1984, just two spots ahead of Michael Jordan. Olajuwon—who played his college ball at Houston alongside Clyde Drexler—would revolutionize the center position, bringing an elegance and finesse of a big man that had never been seen before his arrival.

"I didn't say, 'Let me go open the door,'" Olajuwon told *The Athletic* in 2019. "The moment, this was the opportunity that was available for me, and I was competing, doing all of the necessary things for me to succeed. I've been so blessed to have all these good people around me to help me succeed to that level, where if somebody comes in now, you just don't open the door, you do it at the highest level. International players see that this has been done and they expect it to be like that."

Olajuwon, Dikembe Mutombo, and Steve Nash—yes, the Canadian star point guard was actually born in South Africa— may not have viewed themselves as trailblazers in the African movement to the NBA, but that's exactly what they became. Mutombo played 18 seasons, using his shot-blocking prowess to carve out a niche role and a cult-like following. Olajuwon is a first ballot Hall of Famer. Together, along with such players as Luol Deng, Andre Iguodala, Manute Bol, and Serge Ibaka paved a path for today's stars that have come from all over

Africa, including one of the game's greatest personalities—and rising stars—in Joel Embiid.

Embiid was born in Cameroon and played one season at Kansas for Bill Self—assuredly quite the culture shock—before being drafted by the Philadelphia 76ers in 2014. The 7-footer missed the first two seasons with a foot injury—the latest bigman foot casualty—but has rebounded to be arguably the best center in the NBA in 2020. The transition, as is true for almost every player entering America from outside the landlocked states, was almost a bigger adjustment than the game itself.

"My life is a movie," Embiid said to Spears in 2016. "I started playing basketball at 15, which was in 2011. Just coming to the States, not knowing anything, no English, not knowing anything about basketball. I always say my life is a movie because everything happened so fast. From coming to the States to sucking at basketball and getting scholarships and getting a chance to go to Kansas and getting a chance to be drafted No. 3 to getting injured and getting injured again. And finally, I get a chance to play. All of this in seven years. It's been tough."

Embiid's rise is made all the more astounding by the fact that when he first arrived on American soil, he was missing two key abilities—he did not yet speak English and did not know how to play basketball. The latter, of course, would be quite important in his quest to be in the NBA.

"I got the states and couldn't speak English," Embiid told the BBC in 2018. "Learning English, and how to play basketball . . . it was hard work, but it pays off. At the beginning, when you get to America, as an African player, it's hard. I remember when I got there my teammates were making fun of me. I've always been able to take that as fuel. Nothing is given. You've got to work twice as hard as the Americans. I want for it to be like, 'An African player is the best player in the world.' That's crazy to think about. I don't think that's ever happened. I can't really think of any [team] sports where an African is the best. Even when Hakeem was playing, it was probably MJ, at the time. It would be amazing that that can be said about an African basketball player."

Like many young players from Africa, Embiid idolized Olajuwon, even though he was only eight years old by the time "The Dream" retired.

"I would not go a day without watching it once or twice or three times. Every single day. By myself, any time," Embiid says, recalling a DVD he had growing up of Olajuwon highlights. "That's how I was wired, like, 'I've got to make it.' I just fell in love with the way Hakeem played the game, the way he moved. And then, I learned about his background and it made me fall in love even more because you're learning about a guy that basically started playing at 15, 16 and then I look at myself and I'm in that situation. He played soccer and all those sports. That's basically my story," said Embiid. "You look at a guy like that, you see the way he plays and you just tell yourself, 'If he did it, I can do it, too.'"

Chapter Fourteen

FUTURE, THY NAME IS GIANNIS . . . AND LUKA . . . AND . . .

On June 24, 2019, thirty-three years and one week from the day Arvydas Sabonis's name was called to close out the first round of the 1986 NBA Draft, Giannis Antetokounmpo sat in a comically undersized chair inside the Barker Hangar in Santa Monica, California. In the correct light, his blue blazer sparkled and danced as he waded through the agony that comes with the made-for-TV awards show.

Defensive Player of the Year.

Sixth Man.

Coach of the Year.

The eponymous awards came and went; Antetokounmpo's eyes stayed narrow, rarely darting from their resting position. Before he had departed for the venue, Giannis told his parents that if the night went as they had all prayed for, if he were to be named the NBA's Most Valuable Player for the 2018–19 season, he would mosey up the microphone, stuff his emotions deep inside, and deliver a speech from his head instead of his heart. He believed it so much so that his pockets were empty; he had no folded paper with a written speech, no lists of aunts and uncles and cousins and former coaches to thank. He would stride up to the microphone, cool and collected, then glide through, undeterred from feelings.

Pfft.

It was all a façade.

When Adam Silver—fittingly, as he is arguably the most forward-thinking commissioner in all of professional sports—called his name as the NBA's MVP, Giannis unfolded his comically long body, limb-by-limb, from his chair. When he turned to the microphone and faced the crowd for the first time from the stage, his bold prediction to his parents washed away. His voice cracked. His gigantic left hand swiped instinctively around his mouth over and over again.

"Oh man . . . uhh, I'm nervous," he said, trying to find the proper words for the moment. But before he could go on, the crowd broke out into applause. The cheers came for Giannis, but in so many ways, it was for what Giannis represented. Because although Germany's Dirk Nowitzki had won the award in 2007, and Canada's Steve Nash had done so the two years prior, the crowd knew they were witnessing something altogether new. When Nigeria's Hakeem Olajuwon won the award in 1994, he was in the prime of a career that began at the University of Houston, one-half of the spectacle known as "Phi Slamma Jamma." He had come to Houston a foreigner but had been indoctrinated into the game as a youngster for America to see. He gave hope in a traditional way.

In Nowitzki—who arrived in Dallas in 1998 from Germany— the Mavericks found a young man (he was just twenty years old at the time) who most closely resembled an in-his-prime Arvydas Sabonis. Nowitzki could shoot; he had tremendous court vision;

and he was a match-up nightmare for opponents. Oh, and just to emphasize even more: He could really, *really* shoot. But what Nowitzki needed the most training with—as is most often the case when players come over—was all of the off-court activities.

As Jonathan Abrams wrote in his book, *Boys Among Men: How the Prep-to-Pro Generation Redefined the NBA and Sparked a Basketball Revolution*: "In Nowitzki, [Bill] Peterson found a willing and energetic worker who needed educating not only about the NBA, but also about American customs. Nowitzki was still learning English. The two often ran errands together. [Coaches] would take Nowitzki shopping for supplies and essentials like groceries and a bed."

Giannis, on the other hand, was a true outsider when he arrived in Milwaukee in 2013. He was discovered off of the grainy video, where most scouts agreed it looked as if he were playing in a middle school–sized gym, against opposition that didn't seem much older than that. He was packaged as the ultimate project, a boom-or-bust talent with unearthly appendages and an unknown skillset. He was the definition of taking a gamble on potential.

Fifteen years after his home country of Greece had been the locale to USA Basketball's great demise, the 2004 Olympics, Giannis bookended the sport's global transformation. It no longer mattered what country you were born. It no longer mattered what youth leagues shaped you. It no longer mattered what access scouts had to see you, or how stiff the competition was in your formative years.

Standing in front of the crowd of his peers, some 6,898 miles from his hometown of Athens, Antetokounmpo ushered the NBA into its newest, and most complete, version.

"You know, back in Greece, when they watch the game, it's at 5:00 a.m., 6:00 a.m., and they all stay up and watch the games," he said. By this time, the tears were flowing.

"And they say to me, 'We support you.'"

The next generation was watching.

* * *

As he stood on the floor of the Bucks' first home game in 2019, in anticipation of watching the Antetokounmpo show at an arena unforgettably known as the Mecca, Michael Redd, a longtime member of the Bucks, made the claim that none of his predecessors—from this franchise or otherwise—could truly identify with the prodigy affectionately known as the Greek Freak.

"I've never seen anybody like him," Redd told *Bleacher Report* in 2019. "We've never seen anything like this. The numbers he's getting right now are almost on accident. Once he learns how to play—unstoppable. It's almost like he's from another planet."

Jason Kidd, who coached Antetokounmpo from 2014 to 2018, was more poignant in describing the MVP's skill set.

"Point all," he said. "He's like a plane that just started taking off. He's at 10,000 feet."

Jason Terry, who spent years alongside Hall of Famer Dirk Nowitzki—including winning a title together in 2011 with Dallas—views Giannis's talents through a different scope

"Dirk, in my eyes, is the best European player to ever play this game," he told *Bleacher Report*. "He literally changed the way his position is played. But Giannis doesn't even have a position. He does it all, and he's still learning what to do out there."

Forty-three years prior to Giannis's arrival, the Bucks had taken another player who towered over his competition, who looked almost out of place on the floor due to his length and skills. When the franchise drafted Lew Alcindor in 1969—two years before he would convert to Islam and be given the name Kareem Abdul-Jabbar—the pairing was off from the get-go.

Alcindor was a prodigal thinker who spent his off time evoking the writings of the great black writers, philosophers, and activists. He was a proud black man thrust in an almost comically white city. In 1970, Abdul-Jabbar stuck out like a sore thumb; his prickly personality and shut-off nature didn't help his cause.

In Giannis, the city has found a transcendent star, both in his on-court talent and his off-court way of life.

"I'm a low-profile guy," Antetokounmpo said in 2018. "I don't like all these flashy cities like L.A. or Miami. I don't know if I could be the same player if I played in those cities."

And the combination of the two has reverberated. "They [the Milwaukee Bucks] have breathed new life into the city," Gino Fazzari, owner of the Calderone Club restaurant in downtown Milwaukee, told the *Milwaukee Sentinel*.

"I really don't see Giannis going anywhere," Redd said. "Even in the future. With what he's doing on the court, it's going to automatically draw people to come to play with him. I know people have that stigma about Milwaukee. But it won't be hard for him to attract talent here. I just want a ring when they get a ring."

Giannis, in many ways, is almost too stereotypical. When he first arrived in America, he was overwhelmed by not only the spoils he would receive, but by the rules, too. As Zaza Pachulia, who was born in Tbilisi, Georgia, and played with Giannis in 2013–14, recalls the first time Giannis got his paycheck: "He saw that half of the money was going to taxes. He asks me, is there any way he doesn't pay taxes?"

* * *

Giannis's MVP conquest was the cherry topping for the global rise of the NBA, which had seen a meteoric rise in foreign-born talent over the previous two decades. From the original boom of the mid-1980s, when players like Dražen Petrović and Hakeem Olajuwon were making names for themselves, to generational talents such as Dirk Nowitzki, Yao Ming, Arvydas Sabonis, Vlade Divac, and now the new wave of Luka Dončić, Kristaps Porziņģis, and Antetokounmpo, the league was suddenly awash in new blood.

In 2019, Luka Dončić and the Dallas Mavericks faced off against the Miami Heat and their point guard Goran Dragić. It was an historic matchup; Slovenia's most popular players were squaring off.

"Thousands of Slovenian NBA fans made the 5,000-mile trip to Miami so they could see the country's two most famous athletes square off for the first time," Shandel Richardson wrote in *Sports Illustrated*. "Miami Heat guard Goran Dragic and Dallas Mavericks guard Luka Dončić were at a loss for words after the showing. Their native fans filled American Airlines Arena, at times drowning out the rest of the arena with chants of their names and the country's national anthem. They waited 45 minutes after the game so Dragic could address the crowd."

Ben Golliver tells me that there is one man in particular who—whether it was initially behind the scenes alongside David Stern, or now as commissioner—that deserves a tremendous amount of credit for the explosion of international talent in the NBA. "Adam Silver has made it very clear what a fan of European soccer he is, and the kinds of successes they're having on the field, but also engaging with fan bases and keeping them as very avid fans," he says. "I think a lot of the NBA's big-picture thinking has been oriented around the thought of, 'Hey, we need to be a very global sport, and that doesn't mean going to all of these countries and setting up American basketball academies there, and preaching our way of the game.' It's more about the melting pot approach, where if you've got Luka from Slovenia, and Porziņģis from Latvia, and Embiid from Cameroon, all of those guys bring something distinct and different. The NBA wants to be their ultimate destination, and a place where they can play their game at the same spot.

"You have to convince guys that are going to be multi-millionaires back home to come here and play more games, longer games, back-to-back, thousands of miles from home. That's not always easy to sell."

But that's exactly what they've done, and there doesn't appear to be an end.

However, Silver's visions may not land as he hopes.

Asked about the idea of a mid-season tournament, Croatian-born Mario Hezonja, who played three seasons in Spain for FC Barcelona before entering the NBA Draft in 2015, had some strong words: "*Hell* no. This is the NBA. Come on. They're trying to be like Europe? No way. People are wired differently over here. All these players, we all look up to [Michael] Jordan, Magic Johnson, all of them. And they were grinding, man. There was none of this load management. That's the beauty of the game. I would play back-to-back-to-back. They paved the way for all of us. So for the league to be like, "Forget what they did, let's just do our own thing?" Nah. I think people should adapt their game to ours. We shouldn't be doing anything new. It works. [The tournament] might work, it might bring more money into the league, more excitement, but if it's the best thing, I really don't know."

Ricky Rubio, who played professionally in Spain before coming to the NBA in 2011, told ESPN in 2020 that "It could make the regular season seem not as long as it is. If the tournament is only two months away, it could make teams prepare more. It's hard to say if it'll work or not."

"Every cup means something [in Europe]," says Frenchman Evan Fournier, an eight-year NBA veteran currently with the

Orlando Magic. "If you win the EuroLeague championship, that's the biggest thing."

"The idea is interesting," says Chicago Bulls guard Tomáš Satoranský, who has played professionally in both Spain and his native Czech Republic. "I know how it feels to play in two competitions. The Copa del Rey is interesting because everybody has an equal chance to win. It's a little like the Final Four in the NCAA. So from that standpoint, it would be interesting for the smaller teams who would have a chance to win something. But I think it would be very physically difficult to do it. Players are already tired."

* * *

The future of the NBA doesn't rely solely with the young wave of international players, but the path they are beginning to blaze is undeniable. For players like LeBron James, who grew up with American-born players to idolize like Michael Jordan, the opportunity to be that type of hero for players around the world is not something he takes lightly.

"You never know who you can inspire along your path," he told ESPN after the Lakers beat Dončić and the Mavericks in a November 2019 game. "You hope that you can inspire the next generation. By playing the game the right way, always getting my teammates involved and playing for the purity of the game, I was able to inspire a kid that wasn't even in America. That's pretty special. "[Dončić's] ability to make plays not only for himself but for his teammates, as a rebounder, and just playing for the pure love of the game, it's a beautiful thing to watch."

As Kevin Connor of *The Ringer* wrote after the James-Dončić matchup: "Luka Dončić doesn't have LeBron's athleticism, but if he does take LeBron's place at the forefront of the league, it's because he has the same DNA. Dončić's cerebral game blends footwork, feel, and vision to generate offense against any defense, and he delivers passes with LeBronian velocity and precision. Dončić [said] that LeBron was his idol. 'He's still my idol now,' he said."

Dončić, although not the physical threat that Giannis is, still brings a uniqueness to the game that is nearly unmatched. His ability to stop on a dime, and his unrivaled court vision, do not come naturally to a 6-foot-7 player, especially when combined with the balance and strength to fling the ball all over the court on the move and in a crowd. "His skill level is right up there with Stephen [Curry]," Brandon Payne, Curry's trainer, told NBC Sports' Tom Haberstroh on a podcast in 2020.

Like Curry, Dončić allows you to believe that, with enough work, you might be able to do what he does. His touch and ability to read the game on the fly, though, are probably better understood as superpowers.

"He doesn't have a 42-inch vertical, he's not blisteringly fast, but he uses his smarts and he knows how to use his body to create angles and get defenders on his hips," Ryan Broekhoff, then a teammate of Luka's, told CBS Sports in 2019. "And he's just so smart and so strong when he gets you in that position that you kind of just bend to his will. Whatever he wants to do, he's going to do. Although you try your hardest, he just finds ways. It's kind of too hard to teach. You can try and take things from [watching] it, but to do that naturally is a gift."

* * *

The ever-changing dynamic and political landscape around the globe has not been lost in the sporting world. Dave Gasman, an agent who has represented numerous NBA players, as well as professional players overseas, tells me that may have also been a determining factor in players feeling more urgency to come to the NBA, whereas in the past they may have been more patient.

"The overseas business has changed a lot but has also remained the same in ways. The main difference is it's actually sponsor-driven. I guess on some level the NBA is, in a way, but from a financial perspective, you don't usually have wealthy owners. You have companies that sponsor teams. So, if the economy is down, that means, oftentimes, teams in that league may have down financial years as well. This creates pressure on teams to also have tremendous differences within the same league in terms of financial capability. You might have one team that can pay, that has a $10 million budget. And you may have another team in that league with a $500,000 budget."

EuroLeague CEO Jordi Bertomeu told ESPN.com:

I think that we have to be realistic. I don't like to dream where there is no room for dreaming and, of course, there could be some kind of exception in the future. But we cannot say that the European market, at the level we are at right now, is ready to afford this kind of challenge. The fact that one specific owner can take a very exceptional decision and present this kind of offer [to Josh Childress] does not represent the level of our league. [Bryant or James] would be out of our expectation. It's easy to dream, it's nice and it's cheap but it is not realistic.

If we are ready, at some point, to offer these amounts of money to the best players in the world then I will be the happiest man in the world, but for me, it is much more important to continue growing with stability and a solid base. For me, the problem would be if European teams go to a level of salaries that we can't fulfill. That would be a problem. We've been fortunate, we have never had problems with paying players. That would be one of the worst possible things.

The biggest difference between basketball overseas, and the NBA, isn't necessarily what's found on the court; rather, it's hidden deep in the books of the accountants. Where the NBA league offices will hold teams accountable—*spend at least this much or you're penalized; don't spend too much or you're penalized*—oftentimes in leagues around the world, the difference in competition is more akin to Major League Baseball, where the team willing to spend—or being more capable of spending—walks away with the better squad. "You may have a team in a league with a pretty humble budget, playing against a team with one of the top budgets in the country.

"This financial spectrum is why you see the talent depth disparity from the NBA to leagues elsewhere," Gasman continues. "It's one of the reasons why Americans are high-quality imports to other leagues. But on the best teams, they have high quality European players, and the incoming NBA players can be role players. Top teams in Europe have an NBA structure in terms of personnel, and that's something very positive, and has raised the level of basketball in Europe. The best teams are often star-driven, but role-player oriented. The level of European players have tremendously increased over the years. You have Luka Dončić, who was a great player on his team, and there were other excellent players on his team, and they didn't have [to be led] by the NBA players."

The blending of skills—NBA players heading over, international players coming here—has, in some ways, muddied the waters for NBA players looking to take the next leap. For every Stephon Marbury, who saw his career explode even further in

China, more players from the NBA are seeing that when they step foot in other leagues, no longer are they the main attraction.

"It used to be that if an NBA player went overseas, it was assumed he was going to be a star. It doesn't go that way anymore. A guy can leave the league, go over, and be just another player. There's a ton of parity now. It's not automatic anymore that a guy coming out of the NBA is going to be a star," Gasman tells me. "Asia has really been relevant to NBA players who are seeking financial opportunity. Leaving the NBA to go over to Asia has become a regular occurrence now. NBA players can make NBA-base money in China, where in the past, a player might not do that because he would rather stay in the NBA, not play, but make significantly more than he would in China. Same as in South Korea or Japan."

As Chris Mannix wrote for *Sports Illustrated* in December 2019:

> But Mavericks president Donnie Nelson *knew*. For years he had hopped flight after flight to watch Dončić play. What he saw amazed him. The NBA's bread-and-butter play is the pick-and-roll, and Dončić already showed mastery as a teen. A gifted passer, he could use his 6' 7" height to see over defenses and his sturdy frame to knife through them. At 19 he was averaging 16 points per game against grown EuroLeague men. Whenever Dallas coach Rick Carlisle asked Nelson which player he liked most in the 2018 draft, Nelson told him Dončić—and that it wasn't even close. . . . In Dončić, Dallas doesn't just have the breakout player of 2019—they have a breakout star. His teammates have dubbed him the Matador, a nod to his flair for showmanship.

The fact that players like Dončić have been tasked with leading teams for years—long before they reach the NBA—is not lost on coaches. That they can step in seamlessly at such a young age is a testament to their upbringing.

"I love the fact that he loves carrying the load," Dallas coach Rick Carlisle said of Dončić after a game against Portland on January 24, 2020. "He has great belief in himself, and he's one of these dynamic young players that has the charisma to give his teammates confidence."

* * *

If there's one thing above all else that has been a culture shock to Giannis as his star has risen in the NBA, perhaps it is the relationships he's built with the players he grew up idolizing.

"I didn't expect myself to be getting that close and tight with LeBron James because he's fucking LeBron . . . fucking LeBron James, man. Coming into the league, I never saw myself as one of the best players in the league and being that LeBron type of player," says Giannis. "That's the truth. I could say, 'Yes, I always thought I could be like LeBron James or better or whatever,' but that's not the truth."

Joe Crispin, a former Penn State standout who played in the NBA and overseas, tells me the overall growth of basketball, and the coaching that players receive from an early age, as a big factor as well.

"European players have gotten better, because the basketball world has gotten smaller. But on the flip side, the game has evolved in a way where their skillset and the way they play the game is more valuable in the NBA. There was a total undervaluing of the 3-point shot in the NBA for so long. Everyone would say, 'A three off the dribble is a bad shot.' And I'd be thinking, 'Well . . . why? I can make this shot over 40 percent of the time, so what am I missing?'"

Back in 1988, before the boom of international players dominating the NBA was even a thought, Jack McCallum of *Sports Illustrated* had it pegged. The international revolution, he knew, was coming. But it wasn't just the influx of players; it was much, much bigger. Sure, the players would be the glue that brought together the international audience, but the bigger picture would simply be the NBA opening its eyes to the throngs of fans that awaited them in basketball-fervent nations.

> The NBA has television agreements in 75 countries, on every continent except Antarctica, ranging from the obvious, like Italy, Spain and France, to the esoteric, like Qatar, a small, oil-rich country in the Persian Gulf. As best as the league can figure, 200 million foreign households could receive its games on a regular (60 games per year are broadcast in Italy and Spain) or irregular (14 are shown in Singapore) basis. At the same time, NBA merchandise is being peddled in some 40 countries outside the U.S., so that the wide-eyed Italian lad who watches Magic Johnson on television can run out and buy himself a Laker T-shirt. And what's the NBA's manifest destiny in all of this? Well, you read the itinerary. European expansion. Believe it. It will happen.

Before the start of the 2014 season, Crispin spent time with the Miami Heat before eventually being cut. But even in the short time with the team, he quickly learned the beauty of what San Antonio—at the time the Heat's biggest rivals, and eventual NBA Finals opponent—was doing.

"I spent training camp with the Heat, so I knew the day they were teaching their defense. And the Spurs were just exposing their defense with European counters. They had [Tiago] Splitter and all of the Euros, and they had been taught this way. They had [Boris] Diaw and [Tony] Parker. They were using things they had been taught in Europe for ages. Once that worked, naturally the rest of the league said, 'Oh, we gotta do that.'"

"It was ironic to me, people talking about the Spurs and, 'Oh, this is the Beautiful Game.' I was, like, 'No, they've been doing this overseas for years.'"

The ease of access for scouts and players wanting to learn the game has never been easier. As Crispin details, that in itself may be the biggest factor in seeing the game of basketball continue to develop over generations.

"Now, to click and I'm watching the games," Crispin continues. "As far as understanding the game and learning the game, just the prevalence and ease of being able to watch these games just do change the education of basketball in general. It's also the way the game has moved and evolved to the ball moment and screening actions they have used in Europe for years and years. The NBA has always been known as a copycat league, so when the Spurs won the championships, where they were known for their ball moment, I remember watching them, thinking I knew their countries. I knew them from playing overseas."

CONCLUSION

"Always think outside the box, and always be a kid."

—Kobe Bryant

In the summer of 2018, on the brink of what would become his MVP season, Giannis Antetokounmpo spoke of a workout he had gone through a few summers prior with Kobe Bryant. Those words, spoken by Bryant to the impressionable Giannis, stuck close to him, helping transform his game over the coming seasons.

Those words are both poetic and tragic. Kobe was known first as a kid, bouncing incessantly around the court with almost too much energy for his own good. Later, when the spring didn't coil as much, he looked outside the box to transform. He renovated his shot. He studied angles and tendencies and giveaways. His mind became the spring more than his legs. Because of those tools, as he moved closer to retirement, and as his body began to fail him, his impact on the court remained intact.

But the words to Giannis can apply not just to the game, but life itself. For most, losing your inner child comes about naturally in life. With added responsibility comes less time for imagination. With more structure comes less room for coloring outside the lines, or breaking free from a system.

As the NBA has progressed over the previous twenty seasons, we've witnessed a slow breakdown of the system. Freedom is entering the game. Where coaches once ruled with an iron fist, players, using intuition and their natural abilities, are beginning to run point. It cannot be traced to a singular moment, or player, or philosophy, but it's real, and the game is bettering itself because of that openness. When the Spurs were beginning its dynasty in 1999, at the height of the NBA's lull in scoring output, the prevailing wisdom from couches was that the Spurs were "boring."

But, over time, the beauty of what they were doing crept to the light.

Precision. Execution. Fundamentals.

They were both going back in time and leaping out ahead of the curve. By the time they reached their conclusion in 2014, the Spurs' offense was regarded as a work of art, a pleasure chest for those that dreamed of a break from the norm. Then the Golden State Warriors, helmed by Spurs protégé Steve Kerr, took the reins and completed the league's transformation. It was open. It was free, and fast, and unpredictable.

It was fun.

* * *

The next generation of NBA stars have a blueprint to follow... but it's not one you might think. The blueprint is blank. There are no rules to what they can and cannot do. They've seen the evolution of the sport, and there's no going back. Back then it was Sabonis and Petrović and Divac and Olajuwon. Now it's Dončić and Antetokounmpo and Jokić and Porziņģis and Embiid. And the way the world is evolving, and the way our minds are being opened to how we view each other, the melting pot that is the NBA—much like the entire globe—will only continue to evolve.

During that private talk with Giannis, the youngster asked Kobe, if someone is supposed to be mature while playing the game, how can they remain a kid?

The response was a reminder for us all to never stop evolving. Never lose what made you *you*. Because that kid you once were, that's what kicked off your initial drive to be great.

Kobe's words, like his legacy, should never be forgotten.

"A kid uses his fantasy...you can see a kid being creative and playing. When you're a kid, you always want to learn. You ask questions."

AFTERWORD

In 2004, I walked into a small gym in a remote town of Uruguay called Salto. The floor was some sort of concrete. The backboards were glass, but were so clouded with dirt and dust that you couldn't see through them. And a young high school–aged kid was shooting around by himself.

And he was wearing a jersey. Not just any jersey. An NBA jersey. And not just ANY NBA jersey. A Vancouver Grizzlies Jersey. With "Reeves" on the back.

Yes. Bryant "Big Country" Reeves.

In the mid-90s, Reeves was a pretty big deal. Two-time All-American at Oklahoma State. Sixth overall pick in the 1995 NBA Draft. And just a killer nickname that you had to love.

But, like many players, he failed to live up to the hype and, just six years later, he was no longer in the league.

I had never even seen a Reeves jersey in the States. He had become a nobody. So how did this random kid end up rocking his jersey in maybe the most obscure gym you could find on the other side of the world?

Who knows.

But, it was an image that sticks in my mind that demonstrated just how global the game has become.

I played for eleven years in seven countries on four different continents. Americans were typically signed to most foreign teams as hired guns. They were usually the highest paid and supposed to be the best players (or near the best) on the team. If the team started losing, who was the first to go? The Americans. That is the gig, and guys knew it.

However, the evolution of players and leagues in many countries has been very impressive. In 2006, I played in an All-Star game in Argentina. It was the best Argentineans in the top Argentinean division versus the top Americans in the league. This was not a casual trade basket-for-basket and showboat All-Star game—it was highly competitive right from the jump. Bragging rights were on the line. We didn't want to hear them chirping at us for the rest of the season if we lost. And we were quite confident that we would win. After all, we were supposed to be the best players in the league, right?

Our American team was stacked with talent and athleticism, way more than the Argentineans. They didn't even have their best guys like Manu Ginóbili or Andrés Nocioni, who were already in the NBA.

We played them as hard as we could…but we lost.

The Argentineans played so well together that our athleticism and veteran experience didn't bother them a bit. They seemed so in sync from the start and, frankly, it was impressive to see.

It's truly amazing to see how many gifted international players are now in the NBA. I remember watching an NBA draft years ago and New York Knick fans booing when their team selected a foreign guy in the first round. Welcome to the US, foreign guy. Sorry. It's New York. They'd probably boo the Pope, too.

The NBA has evolved into this worldwide brand that brings in worldwide talent. It's really fun to see fans now embrace foreign-born players. Dirk is, and always will be, a rock star in Dallas. Giannis single handedly put Milwaukee on the map for the first time, it seems, in generations. And I'll never forget Scott Van Pelt on ESPN's *SportsCenter*... "He's not YOUR Vydas. He's not MY Vydas. He's Arvydas...", talking about Arvydas Sabonis, who you couldn't help but be blown away at the skill and basketball IQ of a dude 7-foot, 300 pounds.

I played with the Russian-born Andrei Kirilenko, affectionately known as AK-47, during pre-season with the Utah Jazz in 2006. He had the longest arms and I remember how he did more little things than any player I'd ever seen. Deflections, blocks, rebounds, steals, no-look passes. He filled up EVERY stat possible it seemed, and he could score as well. He would come up with big plays out of nowhere and had this wiry frame that covered so much ground. Plus, he had this spiked blonde hair that just made him an extra-fun guy to cheer for.

At the end of the day, people want to watch and cheer for talented, exciting, and interesting players. Many US players bring that. But, so do many international players, too. They bring a fresh look and feel to the game.

So, while the NBA may have initially had the bigger impact on the rest of the basketball world, international players and leagues will continue to influence the NBA for years to come.

—Tyler Smith

ACKNOWLEDGMENTS

This book proved to be a tremendous undertaking—one I did not fully realize until I was well into researching. The truth is, it would take many books to fully bridge the impacts of all those involved in making the sport of basketball as global as it is today.

The true forerunners of the movement deserve the most credit. From heroes like Henry Biasatti and Boris Stanković, whose pioneering visions forced America to embrace the reality that basketball was a worldwide phenomenon, to the giants like Hakeem Olajuwon, Arvydas Sabonis, Dražen Petrović, and others, who reinforced that with their play on the court. The players who came along after benefitted from their lead; the number of those is too numerous to name, but just flip through the history books and their impacts are obvious.

This book would not have been possible without the fore vision of my editor and friend, Jason Katzman. What originally started out as bantering back and forth about the impact Gregg Popovich and the Spurs had eventually morphed into the wide lens viewing of the growth the NBA has had in totality. He knew more than I did the challenges we would face in harnessing the immense story, and he never let me get too defeated, even in those dark moments writers face when the people on the other end of the line won't pick up, or the emails go unanswered. It's safe to say this book would never have been discussed, let alone finished, if it weren't for the Herculean efforts he went through in making it a reality.

As you noticed through reading the book, I was able to obtain wonderful quotes, anecdotes, and tips from writers around the world who did lots of heavy lifting in years past. Their work was instrumental in tying everything together, and I am grateful for their exceptional writing and reporting that I enjoyed while researching.

To everyone who took time out of their lives to speak with me and to share their knowledge and experience, thank you. That goes double for the wonderful Tyler Smith, who went above and beyond with introducing me to people in his Rolodex.

My parents have never once questioned my dream, and that continued for this. They're the best support system I could have, and I'm grateful every day that I get to have them in my corner.

Writing a book is a team effort. The starting five, in this instance, lived with me through it all. I may have run point, but my wife, Katie, and our three children—Isla, Nash, and Stella—were more than just complimentary players. The time spent scouring the internet during research, hours on the phone doing interviews, and the long nights of writing requires a seamless strategy amongst us all, and we ran that 2-3 zone to near perfection. It took all five collaborating together, and we did just that. Their understanding and patience with me in these times can never be overstated. They are the only four I ever want to team up with.

ABOUT THE AUTHOR

Joel Gunderson is a freelance writer whose work has appeared on the Cauldron at *Sports Illustrated*, *The Athletic*, NBC Sports Northwest, the *San Jose Mercury News*, and the Pac-12 Network. He is a former finalist for the ONPA Sports Feature of the Year Award. The author of *Boise State of Mind*, Joel currently lives in Portland, Oregon, with his wife and three kids.

SOURCES

Periodicals

Abrams, Jonathan. "Arvydas Sabonis' Long, Strange Trip," *Grantland*, August 29, 2011.

Amick, Sam. "How the Spurs Found, Then Almost Lost," *USA Today*, June 4, 2013.

Aravantinos, Dionysis. "The Players Answer. After the NBA Is It the EuroLeague or China?" EuroHoops.net, April 13, 2019.

Arguello, Lorenzo. "A Forgotten Yugoslavian Meat Inspector First Came Up with the idea to Form an Olympic Basketball 'Dream Team'," *Business Insider*, July 10, 2012.

Aschburner, Steve. "Silver Addresses Global Topics Ahead of International Finals," NBA.com, May 30, 2019.

Associated Press. "Dream Team, Barcelona Games Continue to Impact NBA," September 14, 2015.

Ballard, Chris. "Out from the Darkness. Robert Swift's Road from NBA Lottery Pick to Drug Addict to . . . " *Sports Illustrated*, September 21, 2016.

BlazersEdge: The Trail Podcast. "Acquisition of Arvydas Sabonis,"
    June 9, 2016.

Cohen, Ben. "David Stern, Former NBA Commissioner, Dies,"
    Wall Street Journal, January 1, 2020.

Concepcion, Jason. "Watching the Americans. Summer League
    Through the Eyes of European Scouts," *Grantland*, July 21, 2015.

Conn, Jordan Ritter. "Is The NBA Done Drafting International
    Players?" *Grantland*, June 28, 2012.

Conn, Jordan Ritter. "Popo's Boys," *Grantland*, October 1, 2015.

Creppy, Michael. "The Perks of Playing Basketball Overseas," *The
    Undefeated*, June 21, 2018.

Daniels, Tim. "Giannis. I Don't Want to Become 'More
    Americanized' to Be Face of NBA," *Bleacher Report*, March 19,
    2019.

de Jong, Peter. "A Soviet Hipster in the Promised Land," *New
    York Times Magazine*, November 5, 1989.

Deb, Sopan. "The N.B.A. and China Are Showing Signs of
    Reconciliation," *New York Times*, February 14, 2020.

Driver, David. "All Over the Map," *Xavier Nation*, Fall 2017.

EuroHoops.net. "I Would Change the MVP Title for the Gold
    Medal in China," EuroHoops.net, August 3, 2019.

Gaines, Cork. LeBron James' New Coach Explains the Biggest
    Difference Between the NBA and the Euroleague," *Business
    Insider*, August 22, 2014.

Golianopolous, Thomas. "It Was All about Money". An Oral
    History of the 1998-99 NBA Lockout," *The Ringer*, February
    14, 2019.

——— "An Unmitigated Disaster". An Oral History of the 1998-
    99 NBA Lockout," *The Ringer*, February 19, 2019.

Gough, Christina. "Preferred Sport in the United States as of
    2019, by Age," *Statista*, February 24, 2020.

Ham, James. "Vlade Divac's Incredible Journey Leads Him to Basketball Hall of Fame," NBC Sports, April 8, 2019.

Ham, James. "How Vlade Divac Made Global Impact, Paved Basketball Hall of Fame Path," NBC Sports, September 5, 2019.

Helin, Kurt. "Remembering What Went Wrong in 2000-2004 Olympics for Team USA," NBC Sports, August 2, 2016.

Herbert, James. "What the Raptors Winning the 2019 NBA Championship Means to Toronto, Canada and the NBA," CBS Sports, June 14, 2019.

Herbert, James. "That's Pretty Interesting. Everybody Wants to Be Luka Doncic, a Freakish Young Superstar Leaving Peers in Awe," CBS Sports, November 21, 2019.

Holmes, Baxter. "Michelin Restaurants and Fabulous wines. Inside the Secret Team Dinners That Have Built the Spurs' Dynasty," ESPN, April 18, 2019.

Kokkinidis, Tasos. "Giannis Antetokounmpo after Kobe's Death. Life is Short, Keep a Smile on Your Face," *The Greek Reporter*, January 28, 2020.

Kucin Jr., Daniel. "International Players and Unlikely Heroes Shine in NBA Finals," the *Sentinel* newspapers, July 9, 2019.

Jenkins, Sally. "The Hidden Price Steph Curry Pays for Making Impossible Seem Effortless," *Washington Post*, April 8, 2016.

Langlois, Keith. "The Front Office," NBA.com, July 8, 2019.

Lowe, Zach. "Welcome to Manu's Basketball Familia," ESPN, August 27, 2018.

Mannix, Chris. "The Year of Giannis," *The Vertical*, October 24, 2017.

McCallum, Jack. "The NBA," *Sports Illustrated*, February 25, 1991.

———— "Dream Team Still Resonates Long after Dominating 1992 Olympics," *Sports Illustrated*, July 25, 2012.

McDonald, Jeff. "Spirit of '99," *San Antonio Express News*, June 23, 2019.

Maisonet, Eddie. "The Miseducation of the 2004 U.S. Men's Olympic Basketball Team," *Bleacher Report*, September 5, 2017.

Monroe, Mike. "Relationship Building, Hard Work Helped Popovich Rise from Humble Start," *San Antonio Express News*, October 26, 2014.

Nizinski, John. "Drazen Petrovic. Remembering the Star That Didn't Get to Shine," *Bleacher Report*, January 17, 2012.

Penn, Nate. "Dunk'd. An Oral History of the 2004 Dream Team," *GQ*, July 27, 2012.

Reynolds, Tim. "'Our Fans Are Everywhere'. NBA Still Growing Internationally," NBC Boston, October 12, 2018.

Rovell, Darren. "How Nike Landed Michael Jordan," ESPN, February 15, 2013.

Scotto, Michael. "Nearly 25 years after His Death, Nets Carry On Drazen Petrovic's Legacy," *The Athletic*, February 26, 2018.

Sharp, Andrew. "NBA International," *Sports Illustrated*, January 17–18, 2018.

Skolnick, Ethan. "NBA's 'International' Presence on the Rise as Basketball Keeps Growing Globally," CBS Sports, August 31, 2016.

Smith, Sam. "The Overlooked Star That Is Toni Kukoc," NBA.com, January 29, 2020.

Spears, Marc. "Joel Embiid's Long-Awaited Return to the Court — and the Plot Twists along the Way," *The Undefeated*, October 26, 2016.

———— "Gregg Popovich is the NBA's Most 'Woke' Coach," *The Undefeated*, November 9, 2016.

———— "NBA Africa VP Amadou Fall Talks about Growing the Game in the Continent," *The Undefeated*, February 28, 2017.

Sprung, Shlomo. "Inside the NBA's Push to Make Basketball the World's Most Popular Sport," *Forbes*, March 4, 2019.

Tjarks, Jonathan. How the Nuggets Built Their International Basketball Army," *The Ringer*, October 14, 2016.

Toporek, Bryant. "How the San Antonio Spurs Outsourced NBA Dominance," *Bleacher Report*, August 29, 2013.

Walter, John. "The International Conspiracy Behind the Success of the San Antonio Spurs," *Newsweek*, June 6, 2014.

Whitaker, Lang. "The Dream Will Never Die. An Oral History of the Dream Team," *GQ*, June 11, 2012.

Wise, Mike. "The Americanization of Dirk Nowitzki," *New York Times*, February 7, 2001.

Woo, Jeremy. "'Many Shoot, Few Make'. Inside the NBA's First Journey to Russia," *Sports Illustrated*, July 25, 2017.

Zarley, B. David. "'85 NBA Draft Revisited. The Strange Phantom Drafting of Arvydas Sabonis," *Vice*, June 24, 2015.

Zwerling, Jared. "How the Chinese Basketball Association Became the Hot Destination for NBA Talent," *Bleacher Report*, October 29, 2013.

———— "Travel, Relationships and Luck Crucial in Expanding Realm of NBA Scouting," *Bleacher Report*, July 22, 2014.

Books

Abrams, Jonathan. *Boys Among Men. How the Prep-to-Pro Generation Redefined the NBA and Sparked a Basketball Revolution*. New York: Crown Archetype, 2016.

McCallum, Jack. *Dream Team. How Michael, Magic, Larry, Charles, and the Greatest Team of All Time Conquered the World and Changed the Game of Basketball Forever*. New York: Ballantine Books, 2012.

Spehr, Todd. *The Mozart of Basketball. The Remarkable Life and Legacy of Dražen Petrović*. New York: Sports Publishing, 2016.

Documentaries

Last Dance, The, Hehir, Jason. ESPN Films and Netflix, 2020.

Once Brothers, Tolajian, Michael. ESPN Films. *30 for 30*, 2010.

INDEX

Note: Page numbers followed by 'n' with number refer to footnotes.

Silver, Adam, 51–54, 57–61, 167, 171,
    178, 182, 183
Simmons, Ben, 27, 55, 154
Simmons, Bill, 32
Simmons, Willie, xxv
Sixth Man Award, 66
Slovenia, 19, 20, 48, 49, 72, 182
Smith, Dean, 7
Smith, Leon, 123
Smith, Sam, 67, 68, 69, 83
South Korea, 14, 188
Soviet Premier League, 9
Spain, xxviii, 14, 29, 32, 80, 103, 104, 109,
    143–144, 163, 168, 183, 184, 190
Spanish League, xxix
Spears, Marc, 106, 108, 111, 172, 174
Spehr, Todd, 16–17
Spencer, John, 56
Splitter, Tiago, 129, 130, 191
Sports Goods Business, 94
Sports Illustrated, 19, 64, 74, 80, 81, 82,
    149, 152, 160, 182, 188, 190
SportsCenter, xviii, 8, 199
Sprewell, Latrell, 92–93, 96
St. John's University, 9
St. Paul's Apostle, 93
Staniuliene, Deimante, 143
Stanković, Boris, 69–71
Starks, John, 85
Staubach, Roger, 101
Steinberg, Leigh, 59, 60, 61, 78, 88
Stern, David, 2, 4–8, 11, 20–21, 39,
    51, 60, 88, 91, 93, 121, 141, 152,
    153, 160–161, 182
Stockton, John, 46, 65
Stojaković, Peja, 31, 37
Stoudamire, Damon, 95–96
Stoudemire, Amar'e, 135
Stuttgarter Nachrichten, 136
Suzuki, Ichiro, 62
Swift, Rhonda, 159
Swift, Robert, 157–163, 165
Swift, Stromile, 41
Synergy, 25

Ta NEA, 71
Tabak, Zan, 80
Taiwan, 121
"Take Me to the River" (song), 87
Tarkanian, Jerry, 7
Tarpley, Roy, 2
Tatum, Mark, 54
TBS, 152
Terry, Jason, 42, 180
Tesla, Andrej, 19
Texas Christian University (TCU), 27
Thompson, David, 149
Thompson, John, 6
Thompson, Klay, 169
Thorn, Rod, 75
Titus, Mark, 27–28
Tjarks, Jonathan, 25–26
TMZ, xv
TNT, 121
Tokyo Apache, 162
Tolbert, Tom, 136
Toronto Huskies, 23, 24
Toronto Raptors, 59, 95, 165, 167–170
Trent, Gary, 43
Turkey, 109, 163
Turner, Ted, 152, 153
Twitter, viii, 41
Tyson, Mike, 56

Ujiri, Masai, 170, 172
Undefeated, The, 106, 108, 125, 154,
    171, 173
United States Air Force, 112
University of Houston, 5, 38, 178
University of Kentucky, 3, 26, 89
University of North Carolina, 3, 5, 77, 165
University of Utah, 3
University of Washington, xxiiin
Uruguay, 197
US Air Force Academy, 112, 113
US Armed Forces Basketball Team, 112
USA Basketball, 74, 113, 137, 179
USA Today, 124, 125
USSR, 9, 152
Utah Jazz, 34, 47, 89, 93, 94, 199

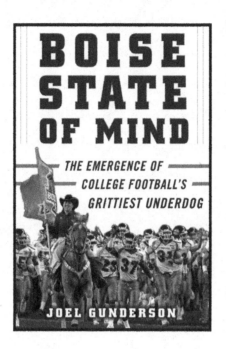

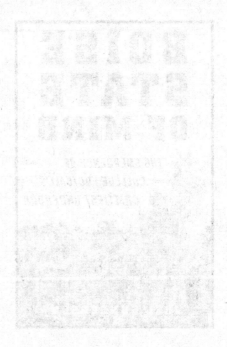